Why Churches Should Not Pay Taxes

Why Churches Should Not Pay Taxes

Dean M. Kelley

Harper & Row, Publishers
New York, Hagerstown, San Francisco, London

1817

FIRST EDITION

ISBN: 0-06-064302-1

LIBRARY OF CONGRESS CATALOG CARD NUMBER: 76-62944

Designed by Sidney Feinberg

To my father,
Mark Millard Kelley

Contents

Introduction

Tax exemption of churches has recently become a subject of interest and controversy as municipalities and even states are increasingly pressed for revenue. Much of the discussion has flourished so freely because unencumbered by knowledge of facts or law. Taxation and exemption are formidable subjects, which many people shy away from or are content to treat in glib generalities. Specialists in tax law, on the other hand, are often happy to keep the lay public at a distance by bedazzling them with the arcane intricacies of the subject—a tactic not unknown to other professions for protecting their occupational territory.

This book is an exercise in popularization, offering an exposition of a difficult subject halfway between the glib generalities and the arcane intricacies—perhaps erring from time to time in one direction or the other. But it tries to correct some common misconceptions (or at least what the author considers misconceptions) and to suggest what the true conceptions ought to be. That is a bold, if not foolhardy, venture, and will probably satisfy neither the specialist nor the uninformed opinion-holder. Nevertheless, it is a needed effort, and if someone else can do it better, let him or her be at it! There is more than enough room for all.

In October 1975, the National Council of Churches, in conjunction with the Wisconsin Council of Churches, the Wisconsin Catholic Conference, and the Michigan Council of Churches, held a Consultation on Churches and Tax Law for church leaders. I organized and coordinated the project, which was jointly planned and addressed by the handful of leading experts on this subject in the nation. I have drawn, consciously and unconsciously, upon their wisdom, though they are not to blame for any misuse of it in the pages that follow. Some of them have been patiently indulgent enough to look through the manuscript, and the author is especially grateful to Father Charles M. Whelan, S.J., Professor of Law at Fordham University, in this respect.

The book is an expansion of the paper with which the Consultation opened, "The Secular Importance of Religion: A Religious-Liberty Rationale for the Unique Status of Churches in American Tax Law." Neither the paper nor the book is intended to be detached or nonpartisan on the subject, reciting neutrally the array of arguments on all sides. Instead, this is a work of advocacy, the advancement (it is hoped) of one particular argument. If the query be heard, "But what about presenting the *other* side?" the reply is that this *is* the "other side." It is offered as a corrective to the prevalent but erroneous "common knowledge" that one encounters on every hand. If someone wishes to reiterate that tiresome viewpoint, let him find his own pen and paper. It will get no free space here beyond that needed to refute it!

Some attention is given in what follows to the importance for American society of tax exemption for all nonprofit voluntary organizations, but the chief concern remains with churches, which have unique responsibilities and interests that diverge at some points from those of other tax-exempt entities.

The main thrust of this exposition is that churches (and other religious bodies) provide a service or function that is essential to society as a whole, and that tax exemption is an optimal arrangement for enabling them to do so. This argument is addressed particularly to those citizens who do not have a present stake or interest in religion themselves—or do not think they have—but who need to understand what it is doing for them and for society as a whole. Ideally, the argument should be made by someone unconnected with religion, but such persons—by definition—usually do not have the interest or "inside information" to know what is going on in the religious enterprise, let alone to write knowledgeably about it.

The author cannot claim detachment or disinterestedness in this cause. He is an ordained minister of the United Methodist Church, has served for a dozen years as a pastor of local churches, and since 1960 as executive for religious liberty of the National Council of Churches, in which capacity he organized the National Study Conference on Church and State in 1964—which included a section on tax exemption. He later worked, over a period of several years, with a study committee that produced the policy statement on TAX EXEMPTION OF CHURCHES adopted by the General Board of the National Council of Churches in 1969 (and which bears a certain filial resemblance to some of the material in this book). He proposed the joint action by the National Council of Churches and the U.S. Catholic Conference urging the end of the exemption of churches from the tax on unrelated business income, which was accomplished in the Tax Reform Act of 1969.

It will be obvious that the author is not an economist, a tax expert, or an attorney. This book does not attempt to deal either with the broad range of tax policy in general or with the peculiar convolutions of special tax incentives for philanthropy (such as charitable remainder trusts, donations of appreciated property, etc.). It should not be viewed in any sense as legal advice, but as a kind of road map, giving a broad overview of the hilly terrain of tax exemption, so that those traversing it will know where pitfalls may be and can consult their own legal counsel. Law is too important to be left to lawyers, and lay persons in the law need to know where issues of religious liberty are at stake in the tax laws affecting (or, more accurately, *not* affecting) churches.

There are many kinds of taxes. Among the commonest are property, income, excise, sales, gift, and inheritance taxes. This book does not attempt to deal with all of these but focuses on the two most important ones: property and income taxation. Of these, the older by far is property taxation, primarily *real* property (land and buildings), though also *personal* property (furnishings, vehicles, jewelry, bonds) in some jurisdictions. Sometimes referred to as *ad valorem* taxation —a term that ought to apply to any tax that is "proportionate to value"—property taxation is highly localized in this country, and thus differs from state to state, county to county, town to town, and is therefore very difficult to describe in generalities. It necessitates such tiresome qualifications as "in some jurisdictions." To try to specify which ones or how many would make this book many times longer.

Income taxation, on the other hand, is easier to describe because, unlike property taxation, there is a national pattern spelled out in the Internal Revenue Code, which, though far from simple, is at least finite and uniform throughout the land. Its main forms are taxation of *individuals* and of *corporations.* Most states and major cities also now tax their residents' incomes, though some are generous enough to permit the taxpayer to use the categories and amounts of his or her federal return for state and municipal purposes, thus simplifying the taxpayer's task and making the federal pattern more or less normative for most states and localities.

This book would not have been possible without the help of the National Council of Churches, which granted the author a sabbatical leave to work on it. Deep appreciation is extended to the Council, to its General Secretary, Claire Randall, and particularly to Lucius Walker, Jr., Associate General Secretary heading the Division of Church and Society, the author's immediate supervisor. The material between these covers, however, is the author's sole responsibility. It does not necessarily express the views of the National Council of Churches, the various churches themselves, or any of their units, leaders, or members. They can all express themselves quite ably, and some have done so, as will be indicated by references in the text.

Some church people have expressed uneasiness with such a pragmatic, utilitarian sort of rationale for tax exemption of churches as is presented here, feeling that the churches' mandate must be biblical and theological rather than legal and sociological. That is true. But tax exemption is not a biblical or theological precept; the churches will attempt to preach and live the Gospel of Christ whether taxed or not, and have done so in many lands under many diverse regimes throughout the centuries, and they will continue to do so. Tax exemption is a legal and sociological arrangement, and the only appropriate rationale for it is pragmatic, utilitarian, prudential. Furthermore, this argument is addressed not just to churches and those who accept their biblical and theological mandate, but it is designed to be useful to them in explaining their situation to those who do *not* necessarily accept that mandate. Therefore, it must be based on data and assumptions that are available to the wider community and which are a common grist for civic discourse.

The discussion of tax exemption of churches—at least in modern terms that have reference to corporate income taxation—is just beginning, and thus far it has been rather one-sided. No coherent rationale has hitherto been spelled out on behalf of churches, and they have been somewhat—and needlessly—defensive, limited either to appeals to tradition or pleas for indulgence.

In reference to "tradition," some have claimed—in rebuttal—that tax exemption of churches is but a vestige or survival of the times when the church was viewed as an arm of the state or an appanage of the sovereign (or both). But that is merely an inference or conjecture, not a causal explanation. No one can find that point in history where some great lawgiver declared, "Come now, and let us exempt the church from taxation, for behold! it is as part of the fabric of the state and a pillar of the throne." There is no time before which churches were taxed and in which we can seek the reason for exemption. It has always been the case, clear back to the priests of Egypt and beyond them into the coulisses of prehistory. The priests and Levites were exempt from taxation, but the written dictum is merely recording a long-existing custom:

> We also notify you that it shall not be lawful to impose tribute, custom or toll upon any one of the priests, the Levites, the singers, the doorkeepers, the temple servants, or other servants of this house of God. (Ezra 7:24)

No reason is stated. One can only conjecture a variety of possibilities. Was exemption an act of recognition of the importance of religion to society (as this book would contend), or of deference to the deity or deities, or of awe of the priests? These historical suppositions are all about equally true or untrue. Who knows? In the absence of evidence, one conjecture is about as good—or as poor—as another.

There were, of course, times and places where churches have been laid under levy to the state, usually in sweeping expropriations designed to counteract the churches' increasing hold on property (see references to mortmain statutes and confiscations at the end of chapter 7). But this kind of action was apparently viewed as a drastic corrective to an excess, and the basic condition of exemption has prevailed before and after.

A rationale need not be a genetic, historic, or causative one. One need not undertake to prove "Why Churches *Were* Exempted from Taxation" in order to suggest why they *should* be. (In fact, the best title might be "Why Churches Do Not Pay Taxes" except that it is static and lacks the normative element, the "oughtness," that is essential to a rationale suitable for advocacy.) Whatever the "reason" for such exemption may be supposed to have been under Solomon or Constantine or Charlemagne or Napoleon, the rationale offered here applies at least to the United States and its revolutionary condition of disestablishment, and possibly to other systems and societies as well.

Chapter 1 states seven common misconceptions about tax exemption and attempts to suggest why they are misconceived. Chapter 2 points out that nonprofit voluntary organizations as a whole are not part of the revenue-producing resources of the nation, but are an important resource of another kind, which taxation might well impair. Chapter 3 focuses on the claims or qualities peculiar to churches, showing where they fit in the vast array of exempt entities. Chapter 4 outlines the central rationale for the churches' claim to a special and "preferred" position in American society and law, while Chapter 5 suggests what qualifies an organization claiming to be religious for that position, offering a test of authenticity that has already excited some controversy. Chapter 6 explores a very sore issue with churches: the legislative restrictions on "attempting to influence legislation," and explains new legislation that modifies that restriction for some organizations, and why churches obtained their exclusion from that law. Chapter 7 suggests several ways in which tax exemption of churches might be modified or limited, with assessments of the threats to religious liberty in each, while Chapter 8 deals with problems allied to fund-raising drives and deductibility of charitable contributions, suggesting how churches should avoid temptations to prostitute their tax exemptions. Chapter 9 points out that—unlike the priests and Levites described in Ezra—ministers pay taxes today like anyone else, or *almost* like anyone else, the difference being a possibly unconstitutional break for clergy who receive a tax-exempt cash allowance for housing. The last chapter raises the question whether the tax code can or should be used as a threat to keep churches and other exempt organizations "in line," exploring the question of discrimination in membership and employment as a case in point. In Appendix A, certain key court decisions pertinent to the subject are described briefly in nontechnical terms, and in Appendix B, certain church views on tax exemption are set forth.

The discussion of tax exemption will go on. If this book enables the churches to hold up their end of the conversation more confidently, it will have served its main purpose.

DEAN M. KELLEY

1

Some Common Misconceptions

Many of our difficulties arise not from events but from the way we view them. We paralyze ourselves with fright by conjuring up bugbears whose existence is mainly in our minds, while disregarding actual perils. Thus an important element in coping with our problems is how we think about them.

There is an extensive literature on "How to Think About . . ." virtually every area of human perplexity. For that matter, almost every writing, every communication from one person to another, has about it some element of advice on "How to Think About" the subject. Some of this advice is good, and some is not so good, depending on the degree to which it "fits the facts"—whatever they may turn out to be—and the degree to which it enables people to cope with their problems constructively, which usually doesn't become apparent until long after the event. So we must sort the good advice from the bad as best we can by the way it matches what we already know of human experience.

This book is an essay in the genre of "How to Think About . . ." It deals with a much-misunderstood area of human affairs for which no adequate rationale is generally accepted and tries to outline such a rationale. That area lies within the broader subject of taxation, but we will not attempt to deal with that broad subject as a whole. Everybody knows "How to Think About Taxation" because everybody pays taxes, just as everybody knows "How to

Think About Digestion" because everybody has to eat.

Although everyone knows "How to Think About Taxation," not everyone agrees on what taxes should be imposed. Some would tax only consumer products, and only at the point of origin; others would tax every increment of value at the point where it is added, and so on into the night. The one trait that marks most people's thinking about taxes is that someone else should pay them.

Self-interest thus introduces a marked slant in all thinking about taxation, causing the whole terrain to slope downward away from the thinker, who considers that he is bearing a disproportionately heavy share of the burden of supporting the commonwealth—a share that could and should be borne more easily by almost anyone else.

As all these thinkers on taxation look down their several slopes of self-interest, there is one thing on which they can agree. That is how to think about the culprit who lies at the bottom where all slopes meet —the non-taxpayer—and that way is: negatively. Challenging the tide of negative unanimity, this book will try to suggest how to think positively about (some) *non*-taxpayers. It will not go so far as to suggest positive thinking about individuals or corporations who should pay taxes and don't, for they should be thought about *very* negatively, but will confine its advocacy to *nonprofit organizations which do not pay taxes,* and particularly to the subcategory of *religious* organizations.

The narrowness of this focus is illustrated by the consideration that, among the relatively few attorneys in the country who specialize in *tax* law, there are very, very few who specialize in the law of charities —or non-taxpayers[1]— and of this very small number (perhaps a few dozen), there are only a handful who combine that expertise with a comparable understanding of the peculiar rights and interests of *religious* organizations.

This uphill task is not made easier by the downward tilt of the very words we must use to discuss the subject. "Tax exemption," "tax immunity," "tax preference"—though originally designed to be neutral—have taken on some of the same pejorative connotations as "tax

---

1. The law affecting non-taxpayers is now much broader than it was when the "law of charities" covered the subject; today it includes also foundations, cooperatives, labor unions, trade associations, and others.

shelter," "windfall," and "loophole." We cannot begin to gain an objective view of the purpose and impact of a system of taxation (and non-taxation) until we can free ourselves—at least temporarily—of such negative preconceptions and stereotypes. We must strive for a brief suspension of self-interest long enough to question some of the inherited fallacies and misconceptions upon which casual discourse about tax exemption turns.

Let us examine seven such common fallacies or misconceptions about tax exemption to loosen up our thinking in preparation for the more detailed exposition of the chapters that follow. We may begin with the phrase "tax exemption" itself, which conjures up a negative "definition of the situation" before the discourse has even begun, and tends to put on the defensive non-taxpayers who have no reason to be under any obligation to defend themselves.

1. *Non-taxation of certain organizations—"tax exemption"—is an abnormal condition which requires special justification or extenuation.* This fallacy or misconception is based on the curiously undemocratic assumption that government has the right, if not the duty, to tax everything that moves and doubly everything that doesn't. Anything that escapes this universal levy is therefore conceived to be enjoying some kind of special privilege or immunity at the expense of the rest of the commonwealth, which must then "make up for" the taxes it doesn't pay.

Now for a moment attempt to put this view of the matter out of mind and entertain another possibility. Suppose, for the sake of argument, that government neither has the right to tax everything nor exercises such a pretentious prerogative, but instead taxes the producers and amplifiers of *wealth,* viz., individuals and *profitmaking* collectivities (corporations). These are the generators of revenue upon which government depends. Other entities, which are not in the wealth-producing category to begin with, do not need to explain why they are not taxed any more than do the birds of the air or the rivers that flow to the sea. Conceivably, government could decide to tax the rivers and birds as well, but the effort would be pointless, since they are not in any meaningful sense producers of wealth.

Nonprofit collectivities are normally not included in the category of wealth producers in Western societies and are therefore not taxed, since each of the *members* of such collectivities already pays his or her share of the costs of the commonwealth, and need not be taxed *again* for the time, effort, interest, and money contributed to collective activities from which he or she derives no monetary gain. That would be "double taxation" indeed, and would work to discourage such constructive endeavors so important to the health of a democratic society. (The next chapter will deal in more detail with the importance of encouraging rather than stifling voluntary nonprofit associations and the advantages of doing this precisely by means of the mechanism of tax exemption.)

2. *Tax exemptions are equivalent to subsidies, and should be granted selectively by legislatures on the same basis as appropriations.* This fallacy or misconception is based upon the same pretotalitarian assumption as the previous one: that government has a claim upon every penny in our pockets, every activity of our lives, every expression or undertaking we attempt, and restrains that claim only by affirmative and magnanimous generosity toward those particular endeavors it (after due deliberation) favors and fosters.

Stanley Surrey, former Assistant Secretary of the Treasury for Tax Policy, has been the foremost proponent of the concept of "tax expenditures" in an effort to get Congress to devote to the tax preferences and loopholes it rather casually writes into the Internal Revenue Code the same care and debate it focuses on appropriations. Such provisions as the oil-depletion allowance, deductions for medical expenses, or the personal exemption, though they merely refrain from taxing, cost the government revenues as real as those actively expended in grants—thus runs the argument, and in a sense it is true and its intention meritorious.

But thinking of exemptions as "subsidies" does not make them so, and indeed belies the history of exemptions in federal tax law. As Boris I. Bittker points out, when Congress wrote the first modern income-tax statutes, the Revenue Act of 1894 and the Revenue Act of 1913, only "net income" was to be taxed, thus excluding all nonprofit organizations, which have *no* "net income." Cordell Hull, author of the 1913 Act, resisted explicit categories of exemption because the law was designed to impose explicit categories of *taxation,* and all not listed would be exempt:

Of course any kind of society or corporation that is not doing business for profit and not acquiring profit would not come within the meaning of the taxing clause. . . . I see no occasion whatever for undertaking to particularize. . . .[2]

As is often the case, however, the Executive branch got the idea upside down.

In administering the new law, however, the Treasury was inclined to treat the particularized list of exempt organizations as exclusive rather than to interpret the statutory reference to "net income" as conferring blanket exemption on all nonprofit organizations.[3]

Bittker concludes:

The exemption of nonprofit organizations, from federal income taxation is neither a special privilege nor a hidden subsidy. Rather, it reflects the application of established principles of income taxation to organizations which, unlike the typical business corporation, do not seek profit.[4]

Furthermore, "refraining from taxation" is not philosophically or operationally equivalent to subsidizing, as will be demonstrated in detail in the next chapter. The most essential difference—with respect to nonproducers of wealth particularly—is that tax exemption, in and of itself, conveys no money whatever to an organization, which cannot build a birdhouse or buy a bathmat with it. The only money such an organization has is what its supporters contribute to it because they believe in it.[5] All that a tax exemption does it to permit the full value of such contributions to go to the purposes intended without diversion to the government, which the contributors already support in their own proper capacity as taxpayers. No one is compelled by tax exemption to support the organization, as they would be by taxation and appropriation. The organization's flourishing or failing is thus depen-

2. 50 Congressional Record 1306 (1913).
3. Boris I. Bittker and George K. Rahdert, "The Exemption of Nonprofit Organizations from Federal Income Taxation," 85 *Yale Law Journal,* at 299, (1976).
4. *Ibid.* at 357.
5. Income from investments, sales, services, etc., all depends upon an original body of prior contributions; it and income from commercial activities, where present, will be differentiated in due course hereinafter, and do not invalidate this point.

dent upon its appeal to voluntary contributors rather than upon the vote of a committee of legislators dispensing funds raised from everyone by the taxing power of the state.

3. *Churches are the only or principal beneficiaries of tax exemption.* In the very week these words were written, there came to hand a typical example of this view, expressed by the president of Union Theological Seminary in New York City, Donald W. Shriver, speaking to a group of businessmen at the Cathedral of St. John the Divine:

> I am told that the largest owners of land and real estate in New York City are churches. . . . If I were a politician at City Hall or a corporation president, I would wonder at the justice of high taxes on business and no taxes at all on so-called non-profit institutions. . . . I shudder to think what would happen to the annual budget of Union Theological Seminary if the City of New York suddenly started taxing us at the same rate it taxes other private property here. . . . I say this out of a sense of personal repentance, in the hope that in the next few years we and similar institutions can find a way to be institutionally repentant.[6]

This statement echoes the sentiments of Eugene Carson Blake, then Stated Clerk of the United Presbyterian Church in the U.S.A. and since Secretary General of the World Council of Churches, who wrote a paper for a top-level ecumenical Consultation on Church and State, published in *Christianity Today,* August 3, 1959, which set the style for this mode of thinking. In it he noted with alarm the increasing property holdings of churches and predicted that they would be subjected to forcible confiscation (as in various countries in past centuries) if they did not voluntarily begin to pay their "fair share" of taxes. In between Blake and Shriver, there have been a number of church leaders and followers expressing similar views.

Dr. Shriver's statement began with an egregious factual error. Whoever told him that "the largest owners of land and real estate in New York City are churches" misinformed him. One supposes that perhaps he meant "the largest owners of *tax-exempt* land," since there are many categories of landholders of *taxable* real estate which exceed the holdings of churches. But even among *exempt* holdings, churches

6. *Religious News Service,* June 25, 1976.

are not the largest. In a friend-of-the-court brief in the *Walz* case (which is discussed in point 6 in this chapter and in Appendix A), the Guild of St. Ives—a group of Episcopal attorneys in New York City writing for the Episcopal Diocese of New York and the Church of the Holy Apostles as *amici curiae*—cited a report of the Citizens Budget Commission on tax-exempt property in New York City in 1967:

> The total value of all exempt property in New York City at that time has been calculated at $15,665,114,130, which if taxed at the then current city-wide basic real estate tax rate, .04957%, would, if the taxes were fully collected, have resulted in added revenues of $776,519,707. The value of the real property in New York City which was tax exempt because of its *religious* ownership and use was $698,339,020, which if taxed at the same rate . . . would have produced $34,617,662 of added revenue per annum. Religious property is therefore about 4½% of the tax exempt property in New York City, 1½% of the total property in New York City.
>
> Owners of tax exempt housing ($2.1 billion), the City Department of Parks ($1.5 billion), the City Board of Education and Higher Education ($1.4 billion), the City Department of Public Works ($1.3 billion), the Department of Marine and Aviation ($971 million), and the combined hospital-health establishment ($1.0 billion)—each then owned more tax exempt property in New York City than do all religious organizations together.

Even if one excludes property that is exempt because it is owned by city, state, or federal government or the huge public authorities, the category of religious exemptions is still not the largest single body of private (nongovernmental) exempt property. From the 1968–1969 Annual Report of the City of New York Tax Commission, Alfred Balk cites figures for exemptions which indicate the following: churches, synagogues, monasteries, convents, etc., aggregated $726,010,645 (this was for a later year than the figures cited by the Guild of St. Ives), whereas private schools and colleges aggregated $801,790,530. Even if one adds exemptions for parsonages ($25,844,325) and clergy ($1,399,400—the aggregation of $1500 reduction of assessed valuation for residential property privately owned by clergy-persons, presumably), the total attributable to religion rises to $753,254,370, which is still less than the figure for private schools and colleges. Both are topped by another category which Balk considers very significant: tax exemptions extended to private persons and groups as "incentives" for undertaking various kinds of building or development desired by the city, aggregating $913,400,000 when one combines limited dividend housing, $80.3 million; redevelopment, $215.9 million; limited profit housing, $290.1 million; railroad exemptions, $268.1 million; and alterations, $58.8 million.[7]

(One needs to keep in mind the caveat that applies to all purported surveys of the value of tax-exempt property. The evaluation and assessment of *taxable* property is a costly and disputatious business that keeps the assessors busy; their estimates of the value of *exempt* property is highly inexact, since it yields no revenue to defray the costs of detailed appraisal. And what standard is—or should be—used? Construction cost or purchase price minus depreciation? Replacement cost or resale value? If the last, what price tag do you put on a used cathedral? Therefore, distrust all supposed estimates of exempt property, by whomever made.)

The figures given above apply only to New York City in the late 1960s, but the relative rank order of categories probably has not changed much since that time, and it probably is not greatly different from the situation that prevails across the country. The aggregate amounts may be larger or smaller, but the proportions within and between the various exempt categories are probably not vastly different. If so, we see that *churches represent only a minor* (but not insignificant) *fraction of the total amount of exempt property in the United States.*

Like other taxes, property taxes are designed to raise revenue for governmental purposes. Unlike the income tax, however, which focuses on net income accruing to the private benefit of individuals, real property taxes focus on the ownership of real estate. Churches do not have "net income accruing to private benefit" in the income tax sense, but they do own real property. Why, then, should churches (or any other organizations, such as the Atomic Energy Commission, the Mayo Clinic, or Yale University) be exempt from property taxes?

The reasons for property tax exemptions vary somewhat according

7. Alfred Balk, *The Free List: Property Without Taxes* (New York: Russell Sage Foundation, 1971), p. 108 and Appendix 35 & 36, pp. 244–246.

to the nature of the property owner. Obviously, it would be futile and wasteful for the government to tax public property such as court-houses and jails. Government routinely grants property tax exemp-tions, reductions, or rebates to businesses that government wishes to stimulate (such as low-income housing projects or new industries that will provide more local employment). In the case of nonprofit charita-ble, educational, and health-care institutions, property tax exemptions remove what would otherwise be a very serious roadblock to private initiative in these areas. If there is to continue to be a private sector in American education, medical care, charitable and welfare activi-ties, property tax exemptions are extremely important—indeed, al-most certainly indispensable.

To say, then, that all property owners should pay "their fair share" is to violate both American traditions and practical economic reali-ties. Taxing nonprofit schools and hospitals would raise the costs of education and medical care without any guarantee of a corresponding decrease in the cost of local, state, and federal services.

In 1970, the United States Supreme Court held that the traditional property tax exemptions for churches are constitutional (*Walz* v. *Tax Comm'n. of the City of New York,* discussed below). The question remains, however, whether such exemptions are desirable. Should the real estate owned by churches and used exclusively for religious pur-poses be exempt like government property, certain business property, and the property of nonprofit charitable, educational, and health-care institutions; or should it be taxed like the real property of well-established and successful businesses or real property held by private individuals for their personal residence, pleasure, or income? These are the questions that must be asked and answered in any sensible, realistic discussion of the property tax exemptions of churches.

Lacking an adequate rationale for tax exemption, church leaders have often tended to accept the characterizations of their critics that they are somehow "free-loading" on the community. Some, in a paroxysm of sentimental self-flagellation, have called their followers to repentance for conduct in which—under a more sensible and realis-tic rationale—there need be no sense of guilt.

4. *Churches are using their tax exemptions to engage in commercial enterprises in unfair competition with taxpaying businesses.* Horror

stories are told of churches buying hotels and factories, farms and office buildings, and leasing them back to their former owners to be run as speculative investments with the great advantage of no longer having to pay corporate income taxes. The prize instance of this kind was the purchase by Rex Humbard's Cathedral of Tomorrow in Akron, Ohio, of the Realform Girdle Company in Brooklyn, New York.

A few of these horror stories, oft repeated and enlarged, add up to quite a scandal, the only defect of which is that it is not true. (a) There were never more than a handful of such instances, and most of them occurred in independent or "free-lance" churches rather than in the major denominations, which did not approve of such gimmicks. (For instance, a Roman Catholic cardinal was told by his lawyer of several such church-owned businesses in the archdiocese. "Are they legal?" asked the cardinal. "Yes," replied the lawyer. "Are they moral?" asked the cardinal. "No," replied the lawyer. "Then get rid of them!" said the cardinal.) During the middle 1960s, the *Wall Street Journal* and the documentary-news department of CBS were looking all over the country for any such arrangements, and they never came up with more than a mere handful.

(b) Most church-owned businesses or investment properties used for purposes unrelated to the exempt purpose of the church pay property taxes like any other businesses. Trinity Parish in New York City, for instance, does indeed own a great deal of extremely valuable real estate on Manhattan Island. It also pays property taxes to the City of New York on all of it that is not actually used for religious purposes (that is, for chapels, cemeteries, schools). Most other jurisdictions also tax church-owned property that is not developed or not used for distinctly religious purposes. (The current struggles are over borderline cases, such as church-owned publishing houses which print both religious and secular publications.)

(c) Until 1969, churches were unique among entities exempt under section 501(c)(3)of the Internal Revenue Code in not having to pay corporate income tax on "unrelated business income." This was the "loophole" which permitted and encouraged the purchase of girdle factories and other speculative investments by a few churches. But in 1969, the National Council of Churches and the U.S. Catholic Conference jointly asked the House Ways and Means Committee to *close* that loophole, and it was closed by the Tax Reform Act of 1969 (with a five-year period of grace for existing church-owned businesses to be phased out, which expired on January 1, 1976), so that the horror stories of the 1960s are not only gross exaggerations but ancient history. It is not often that great institutions ask Congress to end the tax advantages from which they ostensibly benefit, and that historic action should stand as a vivid backdrop to this book. The churches did not want a tax advantage they did not think was right, and they voluntarily took action to eliminate it. How many other institutions in American life can make that claim? (On the other hand, churches should not let themselves be shamed into concessions in a situation that they should consider rightful and proper, which it is the burden of this book to demonstrate.)

5. *Churches should begin to pay their "fair share" of taxes, or at least make voluntary contributions "in lieu of taxes," to hard-pressed municipalities with a shrinking tax base.* This is occasionally heard from a few ecclesiastical romanticists with an overworked sense of guilt and an underdeveloped concept of taxation. In fact, one major religious body, the United Presbyterian Church in the U.S.A., has officially urged its congregations to make voluntary contributions in lieu of taxes to their municipalities after the model of some governmental agencies.

> Congregations [should] be encouraged to take the initiative in making contributions to local communities, in lieu of taxes, in recognition of police, fire, and other services provided by local government. This consideration commends itself especially to well-established and financially stable churches and particularly to those in communities where tax problems are developing due, in part, to the increase in exempted properties for all purposes—educational, governmental, charitable, and religious.[8]

A few years later, the General Conference of the United Methodist Church adopted a similar view:

> We urge churches to consider at least the following factors in determining their response to the granting of immunity from property taxes: (1) Re-

8. "Relations Between Church and State," 1964, p. 16. See Appendix B.

sponsibility to make appropriate contribution, in lieu of taxes, for essential services provided by government. . . .[9]

A few congregations have actually made such contributions—for a while. Other denominations, however, particularly Lutheran and Episcopal, have firmly resisted this trend, insisting that it is inappropriate for churches to make such payments—as though they were the Triborough Bridge and Tunnel Authority—for the following reasons:

(a) Such payments may be seen as conceding the right of the municipality to tax church property (as actually happened in Nashville, Tennessee, when voluntary payments to the City by the Southern Baptist Sunday School Board's bookstores were cited as evidence that the Board could and should pay taxes on its publishing house).

(b) They may create invidious distinctions between churches which can afford to make such payments and those which cannot.

(c) The amount of such contributions may create more problems than they (supposedly) solve. What is the appropriate amount? The same as secular property of equal assessed valuation? Half of that amount? One-tenth? Since virtually none of the few congregations making such payments has come anywhere near the full rate, and the amounts they *have* paid have tended to diminish year by year, should the municipality not prod them a little to increase the amount? In a tightening economy, what happens when the congregation cuts back on its contribution to the city, which then needs it even more?

(d) Gratuitous payments for nonreligious purposes may violate the fiduciary duties of trustees of the church under certain circumstances.[10] The rejection of voluntary contributions in lieu of taxes does not mean that churches are entitled to free water, sewerage, paving, or other municipal services; they should pay for any such services they actually need and use, as will be spelled out in more detail in Chapter 7.

6. *Exempt organizations are given exemption by legislative grace in return for specified public services which government would otherwise have to provide.* The lower courts have often used this glib *quid pro*

9. "Church-Government Relations in the U.S.A." See Appendix B.
10. The foregoing considerations were suggested in 1965 by Hugh R. Jones, Esq., then Chancellor of the Episcopal Diocese of Central New York and now a judge of the Court of Appeals, New York's highest court.

quo doctrine in dealing with questions of tax exemption, and it may have its merits in reference to colleges, hospitals, libraries, parks or golf courses, but it is *not* applicable to *churches,* since government could not constitutionally set up or operate a church to provide the religious service churches provide. Neither can government establish standards of public service which churches must meet to qualify for tax exemption. (In the 1950s, churches in California were required to file annual loyalty oaths on behalf of their congregations to "qualify" for tax exemption, but this requirement was struck down by the Supreme Court.[11] This episode stands as a reminder of the perils of the *quid pro quo* position for churches: that government can decide what services they are supposed to be rendering, and then take away the tax exemption of those which are adjudged not to be rendering them.)

The U.S. Supreme Court, in the only decision dealing specifically with tax exemption of churches, *Walz* v. *Tax Commission,* explicitly rejected such a basis for tax exemption of churches:

> We find it unnecessary to justify the tax exemption on the social welfare services or "good works" that some churches perform for parishioners and others—family counselling, aid to the elderly and the infirm, and to children. Churches vary substantially in the scope of such services; programs expand or contract according to resources and need. . . . The extent of social services may vary, depending on whether the church serves an urban or rural, a rich or poor constituency. To give emphasis to so variable an aspect of the work of religious bodies would introduce an element of governmental evaluation and standards as to the worth of particular social welfare programs, thus producing a kind of continuing day-to-day relationship which the policy of neutrality seeks to minimize. Hence, the use of a social welfare yardstick as a significant element to qualify for tax exemption could conceivably give rise to confrontations that could escalate to constitutional dimensions.[12]

In that same decision, the Supreme Court carefully avoided using the "legislative grace" formula with respect to churches. It did not say

11. *First Unitarian Church of Los Angeles* v. *County of Los Angeles,* 357 U.S. 545 (1958), *Speiser* v. *Randall,* 357 U.S. 513 (1958). See Appendix A.
12. *Walz* v. *Tax Commission,* 397 U.S. 664 (1970). See Appendix A.

that legislatures are *required* by the Constitution to exempt churches from taxation (as the National Council of Churches and the Synagogue Council of America had contended in friend-of-the-court briefs in that case), but neither did it say that they could *withhold* such exemption. It simply found that the constitution of the State of New York did not violate the no-establishment clause of the First Amendment by including "religious" with "educational" and "charitable" as purposes for which property is exempt from taxation.

There is a series of important earlier Supreme Court decisions in cases involving Jehovah's Witnesses which suggests that government may not tax the free exercise of religion, and—by legitimate analogy —the property or income necessary for the same. In *Murdock* v. *Pennsylvania,* the Court struck down a local tax levied upon a door-to-door salesman of religious tracts, saying:

> The power to tax the exercise of a privilege is the power to control or suppress its enjoyment. . . . Those who can tax the exercise of this religious practice can make its exercise so costly as to deprive it of the resources necessary for its maintenance.[13]

The Synagogue Council of America, in its *amicus* brief in *Walz,* remarked upon this quotation:

> . . . property used for religious purposes, including the house of worship, the religious sanctuary, and all that is contained therein are so intimately connected with religious exercise that to levy a direct tax upon the value of such property would constitute a tax on the exercise of religion having the same effect as that tax upon the itinerant evangelist which the Court found unconstitutional in *Murdock.*[14]

There are those who will dispute any contention that the legislatures have the authority under the First Amendment to tax the churches. The Supreme Court has not upheld this view as yet, nor has it rejected it. If any legislature undertakes to levy a tax upon the house of worship, the churches and synagogues will fight it to the highest court. Meanwhile, if the doctrine of "legislative grace" is not a "fal-

13. *Murdock* v. *Pennsylvania,* 319 U.S. 105 (1943).
14. Brief *Amici Curiae* of the Synagogue Council of America, et al. in *Walz* v. *Tax Commission* (1970), p. 11.

lacy" in the full sense, it is at least a "sectarian" doctrine—one that is not accepted by significant segments of society. Consequently, whenever anyone casually asserts that "tax exemption is *granted* to churches," let their unconceded assumption be pointed out and vigorously contested. There are those of us who do not concede that the legislature can constitutionally tax churches; that is an issue yet to be determined.

7. *"Soft money" should never be used for "lobbying."* "Soft money" is a shorthand term for contributions or expenditures which taxpayers can deduct from their taxable income, thus enabling them to avoid paying tax on those amounts. Persons in the 50% income bracket, for instance, can give $1,000 to charity and thus reduce their taxable income by that amount, and consequently pay $500 less in taxes. Thus, they would be giving away dollars that cost them only 50 cents apiece, which is "soft money"—though it will buy just as much as "hard money"—except in one respect. Most organizations which qualify for deductible contributions ("public charities") are forbidden to engage (to any "substantial" extent) in efforts to influence legislation ("lobbying"). Thus the doctrine has developed that "soft money" cannot be used for "lobbying," and the view of the courts seems to have been formulated by Judge Learned Hand in a famous case, *Slee* v. *Commissioner,* in which the issue was the deductibility of gifts to the American Birth Control League. At that time (1930), there was no statutory prohibition, but merely a Treasury regulation against deductibility of contributions to "associations formed to disseminate controversial or partisan propaganda."[15]

Because one of the League's main interests was repeal of laws against birth control, it had been ruled to be outside the realm of "charity" to which deductible contributions could be made. Judge Hand, writing for a unanimous (Second Circuit) Court of Appeals, said:

> Political agitation as such is outside the statute, however innocent the aim, though it adds nothing to dub it "propaganda," a polemical word used to decry the publicity of the other side. Controversies of that sort must be conducted without public subvention; the Treasury stands aside from them.[16]

15. Treas. Reg. 45, art. 517 (1919), in T.D. 2831, 21 *Treas. Decs. Int. Rev.* 285.
16. 42 F.2d 184 (1930). See Appendix A.

In 1934, a specific restriction was added to the Internal Revenue Code at the initiative of Senator David A. Reed of Pennsylvania, who wanted to restrict political agitation designed to advance a donor's selfish interests.[17] Twenty years later, a floor amendment by Senator Lyndon Johnson added a prohibition against interfering in political campaigns, often characterized as "electioneering," so that the entire proscription now reads, in the inimitable prose of the Code:

> . . . no substantial part of the activities of which is carrying on propaganda, or otherwise attempting, to influence legislation, and which does not participate in, or intervene in (including the publishing or distributing of statements), any political campaign on behalf of any candidate for public office.[18]

Congress and the courts seem increasingly to accept the view that only "hard money" (on which taxes have been paid) can be used to influence the political process. Several organizations have deliberately not sought the status of "public charities" under Section 501(c)(3) in order to be free to engage in "attempting to influence legislation," among them the American Civil Liberties Union and the NAACP. In Chapter 6 we will consider whether the restriction in Section 501(c)(3) is constitutional; here we are considering only the fallaciousness of the principle that "soft money" should never be used for "lobbying."

The fallacy of that "principle" is that it has come to apply only to charitable contributions, to causes devoted in the main to the *public* interest. Since an amendment in 1962 to Section 162(e) of the Code, this "principle" no longer applies to expenses incurred by businesses or their trade associations for lobbying on behalf of their own financial interests, which can now be deducted as a necessary cost of doing business. Thus "soft money" *can* be used for "lobbying"—but only if it is in furtherance, not of the public interest, but of private business interests! The Treasury doesn't seem to "stand aside" from that.

The Tax Reform Act of 1976 created some new rules governing lobbying by exempt organizations (new Section 501(h) of the Internal Revenue Code, discussed in Chapter 6). These new rules, however, do not materially affect the activities of churches and their related agencies, because Congress—at the request of the churches—did not make

17. See Chapter 6.
18. Section 501(c)(3).

the rules applicable to them. But the new rules make the "soft money" argument softer than ever, because Congress has now authorized the political use of "soft money," within certain limitations, both by businesses and by many types of exempt organizations.

The foregoing seven fallacies or misconceptions are examples of how *not* to think about tax exemption. It would be foolhardy to suppose that this brief treatment has refuted them all in the mind of every reader. At most, it has shown them to be contested, fitting subjects for argument and dispute, which should be challenged as "sectarian" doctrines (rather than generally accepted axioms) whenever and wherever they appear. But we have not yet considered how we *should* think about tax exemption; to that subject the remainder of this book is devoted.

2

The People's Part of American Public Life

Americans tend to take for granted the rich associational life of the United States, but foreign observers have often remarked upon the unusually prominent role that voluntary organizations play in this country. Alexis de Tocqueville commented in the 1830s:

Americans of all ages, all conditions, and all dispositions constantly form associations. They have not only commercial and manufacturing companies, in which all take part, but associations of a thousand other kinds, religious, moral, serious, futile, general or restricted, enormous or diminutive. The Americans make associations to give entertainments, to found seminaries, to build inns, to construct churches, to diffuse books, to send missionaries to the antipodes; in this manner they found hospitals, prisons and schools. If it is proposed to inculcate some truth or to foster some feeling by the encouragement of a great example, they form a society. Wherever at the head of some new undertaking you see the government in France, or a man of rank in England, in the United States you will be sure to find an association.[1]

He distinguishes between political associations, commercial or industrial corporations, and a third group:

1. Alexis de Tocqueville, *Democracy in America* (New York: Alfred Knopf, 1966), Vol. II, Second Book, Chapter V, p. 106.

Nothing, in my opinion, is more deserving of our attention than the intellectual and moral associations of America. The political and industrial associations of that country strike us forcibly; but the others elude our observation, or if we discover them, we understand them imperfectly because we have hardly ever seen anything of the kind. It must be acknowledged, however, that they are as necessary to the American people as the former, and perhaps more so.[2]

In one of those telling characterizations that take the form of ethnic anecdote, it is said that Americans are the sort of beings who, if three of them fell out of an airplane, would have organized themselves into a society before they hit the ground and elected a president, vice-president and secretary-treasurer!

A trichotomy similar to de Tocqueville's is used in the Report of the Commission on Private Philanthropy and Public Needs, a prestigious private group referred to hereinafter as "the Filer Commission" after its chairperson John H. Filer:

On the map of American society, one of the least charted regions is variously known as the voluntary, the private non-profit or simply the third sector. Third, that is, after the often over-shadowing worlds of government and business.[3]

The Commission then proceeds to try to sketch a "chart" of this "voluntary sector":

The Internal Revenue Service lists, as of June, 1975, 691,627 exempt organizations, groups that have formally filed for and been accorded exemption from federal income taxes. But that number does not include a great many church organizations which automatically enjoy exemption from federal income taxes without filing, nor does it include numerous small organizations that never feel the need to file for tax exemption. . . . One Commission report calculated that a "core group" of traditional philanthropic organizations includes 350,000 religious organizations, 37,000 human service organizations, 6,000 museums, 5,500 private libraries, 4,600 privately supported secondary schools, 3,500 private hospitals,

2. *Ibid.* p. 110.
3. *Giving in America: Toward a Stronger Voluntary Sector,* the Report of the Commission on Private Philanthropy and Public Needs, 1975, p. 31.

1,514 private institutions of higher education, and 1,100 symphony orchestras. . . . In all, counting local chapters of regional or national groups, there may be as many as six million private voluntary organizations in the United States.[4]

Another "chart" of that sector is the *Encyclopedia of Associations,* whose 1976 edition listed 12,866 "national membership organizations" under the following seventeen categories (with the number included under each):[5]

1. Trade, business and commercial organizations	2,837
2. Agricultural organizations and commodity exchanges	612
3. Legal, governmental, public administration and military organizations	450
4. Scientific, engineering and technical organizations	874
5. Educational organizations	878
6. Cultural organizations	1,254
7. Social welfare organizations	777
8. Health and medical organizations	1,138
9. Public affairs organizations	835
10. Fraternal, foreign interest, nationality and ethnic organizations	460
11. Religious organizations[6]	736
12. Veteran, hereditary and patriotic organizations	213
13. Hobby and avocational organizations	681
14. Athletic and sports organizations	449
15. Labor unions, associations and federations	234
16. Chambers of commerce	112
17. Greek letter societies (includes social, professional and honorary)	326

There is an eighteenth category also: 719 "missing" organizations—those which had been listed in previous years but can no longer be located, yet are not definitely known to be defunct. This *Encyclopedia's* listing is far from complete, however, since it has no exhaustive mechanism for locating *all* national organizations, and must depend upon their willingness—once they have been identified—to supply informa-

4. *Ibid.,* p. 36.
5. *Encyclopedia of Associations,* Vol. I, 10th edition (Detroit: Gale Research Co., 1976), Table of Contents.
6. Curiously, a few national religious bodies are listed, but most are not, nor, of course, are their regional judicatories or local congregations, so that "churches" as such are hardly represented in this catalog at all.

tion. The *Encyclopedia* does give us, however, a suggestion of the breadth, diversity, and turnover in the world of organizations.

Whether the United States is unique in the proliferation of its voluntary associations, and however they may be categorized, they form a vital and dynamic element in which individuals may participate at will in order to attain objectives which neither government nor business is attaining or which, perhaps, neither *can* attain. It is in a real sense the *people's* part of American public life, for by freely combining together, self-selecting groups of like-minded persons can take the initiative to meet common needs or pursue shared interests.

Perhaps this pattern of collective self-reliance grew out of the frontier experience in American history, when settlers who had outdistanced government and industry had to rely on what they and their neighbors could accomplish together. The history of the nation would be entirely different—and incomparably poorer—without such organized voluntary efforts. It was the great voluntary movements of the nineteenth century that founded schools and colleges, organized hospitals and other charities, abolished dueling and slavery, formed labor unions, struggled for woman suffrage and other civil rights, and gave collective expression to every kind of enthusiasm, dissatisfaction, and concern.

Similar surgings of citizen initiative arise today, as in the consumer and the environmentalist movements, which have spawned dozens of important new organizations: the Sierra Club, Friends of the Earth, and so on. Whenever a need is felt, a wrong is seen, a hope is envisioned, citizens can mobilize around it and bring their shared objectives to fulfillment. Without such vigorous voluntary organizations, society would be an amorphous mass of isolated, and therefore weak, individuals—which is apparently what some people would like, for such a society would be much easier to manipulate and control.

Captains of the coal industry, for instance, would probably prefer not to have the foes of strip mining organizing themselves to protect the environment. From the viewpoint of those who benefit from the present arrangement of society, every voluntary organization is a potential troublemaker, and so should be identified, registered, scrutinized, and regulated—in the "public interest," of course. But the real public interest runs the other way, in the direction of independent centers of citizen initiative—the more, the merrier—for they give to democracy its vigor and reverberance. They provide the basis for resisting an oppressive government and correcting its excesses. It is not the responsibility of government to supervise the associational life of the populace; quite the contrary: it is the prerogative of the people, through their voluntary organizations, to scrutinize and stimulate, correct and countervail their government.

The willingness of citizens to "get together" to work for the betterment of the community and nation is a priceless and irreplaceable resource, which the government could not supply or synthesize even if it paid every citizen by the hour to go to meetings. But it is not necessary for government to subsidize these activities. It is enough if it simply gets out of the way and leaves them alone, which is precisely what the First Amendment requires: that "Congress shall make no law . . . abridging . . . the right of the people peaceably to assemble [that is, to associate together] and to petition the Government for a redress of grievances"—which presumably means to make their wants and expectations known to the public servants they elect and employ.

One way in which government commendably "gets out of the way" and lets voluntary organizations perform their important work is by "exempting" them from taxation. As we noted in the preceding chapter, "exemption" is a confusing term, since such nonprofit, non-wealth-producing entities are not normally part of the revenue system to begin with. But there are those who, seeing (for instance) the non-taxpaying real estate of the National Geographic Society, the National Education Association, and the American Chemical Society clustered at the intersection of 16th and M streets in Washington, D.C., begin to fulminate about taxing them. Sometimes they modulate this threat by suggesting that some of the taxes realized be returned to these organizations in the form of grants or payments for services —if, indeed, their services are worthy of public support. This, they claim, would be a more straightforward and public-spirited way to go about it. Let all pay taxes, they suggest, and then the legislature can dispense the funds to those institutions which perform services of genuine value to the whole public.

On the contrary, this would be a perniciously wrong-headed and destructive way to go about it! All *do* pay taxes already. That is, all citizens pay what is presumably their fair share of the costs of the commonwealth. To tax them again for participation in voluntary organizations from which they derive no monetary gain would be "double taxation" indeed, and would effectively serve to discourage them from devoting time, money, and energy to organizations which contribute to the upbuilding of the fabric of democracy.

For them to receive back as grants or other payments some of the taxes thus collected in recognition of whatever activities were considered worthy of public support by those currently in office would be no great boon. When one considers the burdens that go with governmental subsidies—the detailed applications, the voluminous reports, the recurrent audits, the multiplying regulations and requirements, the periodic threat of reduction or nonrenewal—one may question whether such support is worth the price. More important, one may wonder to what extent the recipient organization remains a truly "voluntary" and independent agent of its members' interests.

Several universities have recently discovered that federal subsidies —which, a few years ago, they boasted came to them "with no strings attached"—have whole festoons of long and constricting "strings" on them after all—in the form of newly adopted regulations about admissions policies, coeducational athletic programs, restrictions on disciplining of students, etc., etc., and they will discover even more strings in the future. The effect of such requirements—each of which may be meritorious in its own right—is to make the formerly "private" university less and less distinguishable from a "public" or state university.

The only way to insure that an organization or an institution remains responsive to its members' interests is for them to pay the bills rather than trying to get someone else to pay them. There is no truer generalization in human affairs than "who pays the piper calls the tune." When a private voluntary institution accepts tax support, it is to that extent taking all of us in the taxpaying jurisdiction into partnership. It can no longer "cater" to the particular traits and interests of its self-selecting membership, but must be equally available to all.

Some social-welfare agencies have assured themselves that relying on governmental support of various kinds would not really change their character or purpose if it did not exceed 40% of their total budget—or 60%—or 80%—or whatever their current rate of dependence happened to be—which nevertheless increased in succeeding years despite such brave resolves. But the right of government to regulate what it supports follows *every* tax dollar. The regulations promulgated by the Department of Health, Education and Welfare apply to every institution receiving federal money, irrespective of what proportion that money is to its total income.

The courts are currently struggling to determine what degree of subsidy makes a previously private institution in effect a part of government so that citizens as taxpayers have enforceable claims against it for violations of their constitutional rights. One court held in 1963 that a hospital's having accepted Hill-Burton grants and having participated in the state plan under which they were allotted clothed it sufficiently with the quality of "state action" that it could not exclude black physicians from use of its facilities *(Simkins* v. *Moses H. Cohn Memorial Hospital*[7]*),* but another court has held more recently that Hill-Burton grants did not sufficiently imbue a private hospital in Montana with the quality of "state action" that a citizen could claim damages against it because of its refusal to perform an operation forbidden by its code of ethics *(Taylor* v. *St. Vincent's Hospital*[8]*).* However this struggle may be resolved, it seems that the reach of taxpayers' claims against tax-subsidized private institutions, though they may not be further extended, are unlikely to be much reduced.

Private voluntary organizations which receive tax subsidies are no longer as "private" as they were, and indeed may have become quasi-public, often without recognizing that fact until too late. What is meant by "too late"? Can they not give up the "King's shilling" and recover their autonomy? That may be easier said than done, especially if—as in the case of hospitals or colleges—the grant of tax funds has been built into a wing or dormitory. Yet even if government money is only a component in the current-expense budget, it may be no easier to "swear off." Organizations grow and flourish in ways that are not too dissimilar to trees. Excavations of the root systems of trees have found them often to be clustered around various sources of water or nutrition in their vicinity (such as sewer pipes). Sudden drastic

7. 323 F.2d 959, 4th Cir. 1963.
8. 523 F.2d 75, 1975.

changes in the flow of the tree's nourishment can result in its death because it cannot regenerate a new root system overnight.

Similarly, an organization develops its shape, functions, abilities, over the years in response to certain resources and with the expectation that they will continue to flow. It is often severely traumatic—if not actually impossible—to cut off or to eschew the support from a substantial source which has nourished the work for years—not just because of the economic dislocation but because the arrangement has been so generally accepted and expected by the organization's members that they are unlikely to question it or to imagine any other way to go. Thus subsidies create strong symbiotic relationships or dependencies that are not easy to break, and in some cases (as where a "trust" or other structure has been created) may be irreversible.

The beauty of "tax exemption" as an arrangement for encouraging voluntary organizations is that it does not entail the kinds of entanglements and dependencies just described. At least it does not oblige government to examine, inspect, evaluate, compare, audit, standardize, regulate, or control such organizations, as would be the case if they were subsidized. Rather than attempting to assess their worth to the public as a basis for determining the degree of subsidy they deserve, government—by the mechanism of tax exemption—allows the *public* to make that evaluation and decision directly by the degree to which interested persons support the various organizations by their voluntary contributions. It is a wonderfully simple and self-implementing process, which avoids the necessity for another vast federal bureaucracy the size of the Pentagon: the Office for Subsidizing the Worthy Activities of Voluntary Organizations (OSWAVO).

The U.S. Supreme Court, in discussing tax exemption of churches, has clearly distinguished between exemption and subsidy:

> Obviously a direct money subsidy would be a relationship pregnant with involvement and, as with most governmental grant programs, could encompass sustained and detailed administrative relationships for enforcement of statutory or administrative standards, but that is not this case. . . . The government does not transfer part of its revenue to churches but simply abstains from demanding that the church support the state. No one

has ever suggested that tax exemption has converted libraries, art galleries, or hospitals into arms of the state or employees "on the public payroll."[9]

To summarize the operational distinctions between *subsidy* and *tax exemption:*

1. In a tax exemption, *no money changes hands* between government and the organization. There is no financial transaction with applications, checks, warrants, vouchers, receipts, accounting, or audits; ". . . government does not transfer part of its revenue. . . ."

2. A tax exemption, in and of itself, *does not provide one cent* to an organization. Without contributions from its supporters, it has nothing to spend. Government cannot create or sustain—by tax exemption —any organization which does not attract contributions on its own merits.

3. The *amount* of a subsidy is determined by the legislature or an administrator; there is no "amount" involved in a tax exemption because it is "open-ended"; the organization's income is dependent solely on the generosity of its several contributors, each of whom decides freely and individually how much he or she will give.

4. Consequently, there is *no periodic legislative or administrative struggle* to obtain, renew, maintain, or increase the amount, as would be the case with a subsidy; political allegiances are not mobilized to support or to oppose it; the energies of the organization are not expended in applying for, defending, reporting, qualifying, undergoing audits and evaluations, etc., and the resources of government are not expended in administering them.

5. A subsidy is not *voluntary* in the same sense that tax-exempt contributions are. When the legislature taxes the citizenry and appropriates a portion of the revenues as a subsidy to an organization, the individual citizen has nothing determinative to say as to the amount of the subsidy or the selection of the recipient. (Citizens may testify at hearings on such matters and even bring about the defeat of legislators with whom they disagree, but that does not make their "contribution" to the subsidized organization at the time any less compulsory.)

6. A tax exemption does not convert the organization into an agency of "state action," whereas a subsidy—in certain circumstances

9. *Walz* v. *Tax Commission,* 397 U.S. 644 (1970).

—may. ("No one has ever suggested that tax exemption has converted libraries, art galleries, or hospitals into arms of the state or employees 'on the public payroll.' ")

But there is more that government does to "get out of the way" of voluntary organizations. In addition to tax exemption, some organizations benefit from contributions which donors can deduct from their taxable income before paying income tax. Among them are the organizations that are exempt from income tax under Section 501(c)(3)[10] of the Internal Revenue Code. (There are many other categories of tax-exempt organizations—Section 501(c) alone has 19 subdivisions —contributions to most of which are *not* deductible. When an organization "loses its tax exemption," what is usually meant is *not* that *it* loses its *tax* exemption, since it usually qualifies for continued exemption from corporate income tax under Section 501(c)(4) or one of the other categories of Section 501(c), but that its contributors are no longer able to deduct contributions to it from their taxable income.)

Deductibility of contributions is a significant incentive to contributors, particularly those in higher income brackets, and it is justified by the consideration that they do not benefit personally from the contribution in the way that they would from dues paid to a labor union (which is itself exempt under Section 501(c)(5)), shares in a credit union (which is exempt under Section 501(c)(14)(A)), or membership fees in a chamber of commerce (Section 501(c)(5)) or a recreational club (Section 501(c)(7)). "Deductibility" means that not only does the government not claim a share of the contributions made to an organization *after* they reach the organization, but it abstains from

10. Technically, Section 170, not Section 501(c)(3), governs the deductibility of contributions. For purposes of the present discussion, however, it is important to note the various types of organizations that are exempt under Section 501(c). Section 170 makes contributions to *some* of these organizations deductible. The largest and most important group of 501(c) exempt organizations benefiting from the deductibility of contributions is the Section 501(c)(3) class, which includes churches, hospitals, educational institutions, museums, symphony orchestras and a host of other nonprofit organizations. The only type of Section 501(c)(3) organization, contributions to which are not deductible, is an organization dedicated to testing for public safety. The state and federal governments, organizations of war veterans, fraternal societies, and nonsectarian cemetery companies are not Section 501(c)(3) organizations, but contributions to them are deductible under the circumstances prescribed in Section 170(c) of the Internal Revenue Code.

taxing the donor on them *before* they reach the organization.

The Filer Commission Report gives this rationale for the charitable deduction:

> . . . the charitable deduction is a philosophically sound recognition that what a person gives away simply ought not to be considered as income for purposes of imposing an income tax. There is no fixed definition of income; it is a concept that acquires meaning by the context in which the term is used. In the context of personal income taxation, the Commission believes it is appropriate to define income as revenue used for personal consumption or increasing personal wealth and to therefore exclude charitable giving because it is neither. . . . We think it entirely appropriate, in other words, for the person who earns $55,000 and gives $5,000 to charitable organizations to be taxed in exactly the same way as the person who earns $50,000 and gives away nothing.[11]

In order to strengthen the voluntary sector, in fact, the Commission recommended that even greater incentives to charitable giving be written into the tax code, such as permitting the many taxpayers who take the "standard deduction" rather than itemizing all their deductions to claim deductions for itemized charitable contributions over and above the standard deduction. The Commission also recommended that families with incomes under $15,000 a year be allowed to deduct *twice* the amount of their charitable contributions, and families with incomes between $15,000 and $30,000 be allowed to deduct 150% of what they contribute to charities, a proposal that doesn't entirely square with the Commission's rationale outlined above—that charitable contributions are not truly "income." Under this recommendation, if written into law, donors in the lower income brackets would not only be able to exclude contributions from taxable income (which they can do now), but could exclude an additional amount as well—a kind of "matching" tax credit, in which the government would match each dollar contributed with another dollar on which the donor would otherwise have to pay taxes.

The Filer Commission may not see all of its recommendations written into law, but its prestigious report may serve as an "anchor to windward" to prevent the elimination of some of the present incen-

11. *Giving in America*, p. 128.

tives to charitable giving and encouragements of voluntary organizations. The theme of this chapter is one that supports the basic concerns of the Filer Commission in urging every just and legitimate encouragement which the nation's tax policy can give to voluntary organizations.

Some aspects of the tax deductibility of charitable donations are designed to be particularly appealing to affluent persons capable of making "pace-setting" contributions to large fund-raising campaigns. These aspects include the special treatment of gifts of appreciated property (such as stock or real estate), which, under certain circumstances, are deductible at current market value rather than at the original cost to the donor. There are also provisions for deferred giving, such as "charitable remainder trusts" (Section 664 of the Internal Revenue Code), under which money or property can be put in trust by a donor to go to a charitable organization at death, with the interest or an annuity paid to the donor during his or her lifetime. This book does not concern itself with such arrangements, and neither advocates nor opposes them.

3

The Special Claims of Churches

The main focus of this book is on the unique status of churches in American tax law. We have approached the subject by way of the broader category of voluntary nonprofit organizations as a whole, since many of the considerations that apply to them also apply to churches, such as the right to assemble (associate) freely. But churches, in addition to the rights and freedoms they share with voluntary organizations, have special claims to make that are peculiar to themselves and that are based upon considerations that do not apply to other organizations. What those considerations are, and why they justify the churches' claims, will occupy the next two chapters. But it may be helpful in focusing upon the churches to visualize where they fit within the broad "chart" of tax-exempt entities we considered in the preceding chapter.

As we approach the scene, we see the figure of "government" standing astride two solid blocks of revenue, one representing individuals and the other profit-making corporations. Nearby grows a fragile flower, which represents non-taxed entities that are by their very nature not part of the revenue base, though they are nourished by the effluvia of voluntary contributions from the individuals and corporations in that base.

Some people may be distressed by references to "government" as something separate and apart from the populace in general. "In a democracy," they protest, "we *are* the government. It is not our

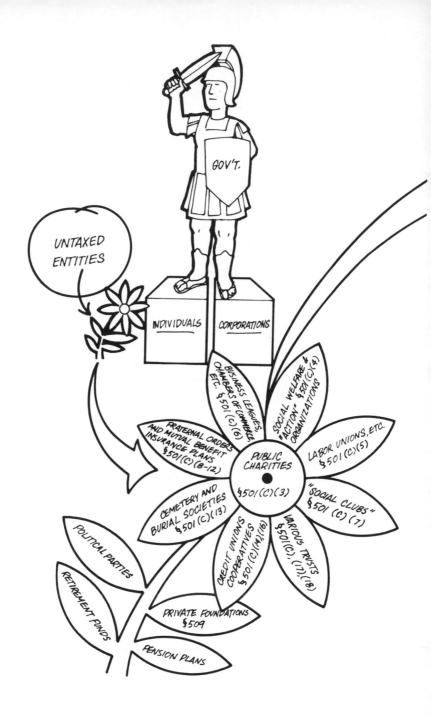

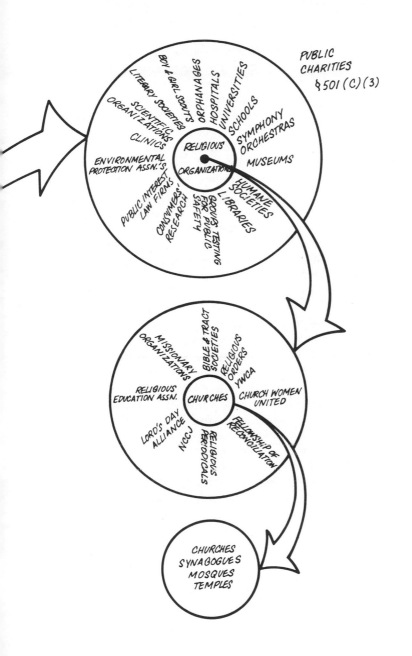

PUBLIC
CHARITIES
§ 501 (C) (3)

PUBLIC CHARITIES § 501 (C) (3)

BOY & GIRL SCOUTS
ORPHANAGES
HOSPITALS
UNIVERSITIES
SCHOOLS
LITERARY SOCIETIES
SCIENTIFIC ORGANIZATIONS
CLINICS
SYMPHONY ORCHESTRAS
ENVIRONMENTAL PROTECTION ASSN.'S
MUSEUMS
RELIGIOUS ORGANIZATIONS
HUMANE SOCIETIES
PUBLIC INTEREST LAW FIRMS
CONSUMERS' RESEARCH
GROUPS TESTING FOR PUBLIC SAFETY
LIBRARIES

MISSIONARY ORGANIZATIONS
BIBLE & TRACT SOCIETIES
RELIGIOUS ORDERS
YWCA
RELIGIOUS EDUCATION ASSN.
CHURCHES
CHURCH WOMEN UNITED
LORD'S DAY ALLIANCE
NCCJ
RELIGIOUS PERIODICALS
FELLOWSHIP OF RECONCILIATION

CHURCHES
SYNAGOGUES
MOSQUES
TEMPLES

adversary but our employee." In a civics-book sense, this is true. But it is not an adequate picture from the perspective of sociology or political science—or of aggrieved individuals or groups seeking to obtain redress from their fellow citizens via the agencies of government. A more accurate picture would recognize that the organizations of government and the persons who occupy them have their own distinctive functions, resistances, and receptivities—both formal and informal—which determine the working of governmental processes in ways not always consonant with the wishes or expectations of the populace at large. This is said neither to praise nor blame but to suggest a certain degree of momentum or functional autonomy in "government" that makes it distinguishable from other institutions and the whole society.

The non-taxable "flower" in our visualization is composed of many varieties of entities, represented by the leaves and petals, including "social-welfare" or "action" organizations (Section 501(c)(4)), labor unions and trade associations, clubs, lodges, recreation groups, cooperatives, pension plans and retirement funds, various trusts and endowments, private foundations, and political parties. This is by no means a complete list, but it suggests the vast range of non-taxed entities and some of the salient types. None of these pays taxes on its corporate income from contributions, though they do on profits from commercial activities (such as the proceeds from paid advertisements in the journal of a trade association). Most of them are not eligible to receive deductible contributions. Most (except for "private foundations") are free to "attempt to influence legislation" or to support or oppose political candidates; in fact, that is what political parties exist to do.

In the center of the flower is a favored group called "public charities." They are described in Section 501(c)(3) of the Internal Revenue Code as organizations whose purposes are exclusively "religious, charitable, scientific, testing for public safety, literary or educational . . . or for the prevention of cruelty to children or animals." (Though "charitable" is listed as one of the several exempt purposes, it is also considered to describe the entire category. That is, though hospitals, schools, humane societies, boy or girl scouts, museums, symphony orchestras, libraries, and public-interest law firms may each fall under one or another of the purposes listed, they are all considered in a more general sense to be "charitable" organizations, in that they are supported mainly by voluntary contributions from persons seeking thereby to advance the general good rather than their own private interests.)

This category is called "favored" because those who make contributions to such organizations (except those devoted to testing for public safety) can deduct them from their taxable income (up to 20% of that income in some cases, up to 50% in others). This attribute, which we call for brevity's sake "deductibility"—though that term properly applies to the gift and to the giver's income tax rather than to the organization to which it is given—is highly coveted, and many organizations aspire to it which do not qualify, and others lose it when they cease to qualify. In one respect, however, this group is not so favored: those organizations enjoying deductibility are very limited in what they can do in the way of "attempting to influence legislation" and entirely prohibited from supporting or opposing candidates for public office. (Some organizations reluctantly eschew deductibility in order to be able to do these things, such as the Friends Committee on National Legislation, the American Civil Liberties Union, and the NAACP; and others have lost it for engaging in them, such as Americans United for Separation of Church and State.)

In the center of our diagram of "public charities" is a group called "religious organizations," which includes Bible societies, religious orders, Church Women United, missionary societies, the Fellowship of Reconciliation, the YWCA, the Woman's Christian Temperance Union, the National Catholic Education Association, and many others which, though not themselves churches or components of churches, are ancillary or auxiliary to them, or channel and respond to religious interests unconnected with any church.

At the very center of this circle is a favored group of organizations that are not only "religious" but are engaged in the "whole" practice of religion: churches, synagogues, temples, mosques, etc. (which is what is ordinarily meant wherever the term "church" is used in the tax code). That is, they are the central repositories of religious activity, from which may flow many kinds of partial or peripheral religious interests or ministrations. Thus a missionary society or a Bible society or a church musicians' guild or an association of religious publishers might embody one or a few aspects of religion but would not be itself a *church,* nor would all of them together constitute a *church.* They are often spawned by churches, but they rarely spawn a church.

Churches as such are not separately identified in Section 501(c)(3), but elsewhere in the Code they are referred to usually as "churches, conventions or associations of churches." This category is specially "favored" in at least the following respects (there are others as well, not listed here):

a. It is listed first in the catalog of organizations contributions to which are deductible from taxable income (Section 170(b)(1)(A)(i));

b. It is given a mandatory exception from the presumption of being a "private foundation" (Section 508(c)(1)(A));

c. It is given a mandatory exception from the requirement that most (other) Section 501 organizations must file annual informational returns (Form 990) with the Internal Revenue Service (Section 6033(a)(2)(A));

d. The Internal Revenue Service is limited in the auditing or examining it may undertake of such organizations (Section 7605(c)).

The remainder of this book will focus on this highly favored category, "churches, conventions or associations of churches." One reason they are distinguishable from other exempt organizations is that, in addition to embodying activities protected by the First Amendment's guarantees of freedom of speech, press, assembly, and petition —as all exempt organizations do—churches also embody the activity protected by the First Amendment's initial clauses, the free exercise of religion and its non-establishment.

It is important to note, of course, that the First Amendment mentions, not "churches," but "religion," and it has been rightly pointed out that there is much religion that is not embodied in or identified with churches, which is equally protected by the First Amendment, and that not everything churches may do is, or should be, covered by the cloak of the First Amendment. That is all true, and should be borne in mind throughout the ensuing exposition. Nevertheless, if one were to look for the most visible, extensive, and enduring collective manifestations of the "free exercise of religion" in this country, where else would one look but to the institutions which inculcate, disseminate, amplify, and perpetuate religious behavior?

There are religious symbols, beliefs, practices, and references to be found elsewhere, to be sure. They are scattered throughout the whole American society and every other society. But these do not in themselves—or all of them together—constitute a going religion capable of propagating and perpetuating itself and spawning derivative movements across the centuries. That requires an ongoing community of faith with its revered teachings, sacred rites and sacraments, and specialized teachers, priests, or other functionaries trained in the belief and practice of the faith. It is not an easy process to get started, nor an easy one to stop, though it can be diverted, degraded, or distorted, as we shall see in the next chapter. There is no living religion without an ongoing community of faith—a "church"—to carry it on. In that sense, churches are an important and indispensable part of whatever it is the first two clauses of the First Amendment are designed to protect under the rubric of "religion."

"Religion" is unique among the activities protected by the First Amendment because, not only is its "free exercise" guaranteed, but the government is forbidden to "establish" it. The wording was originally designed to prevent Congress from establishing a *national* church *or* interfering with the several *state* establishments then existing: "Congress shall make no law *respecting* an establishment of religion . . ." (emphasis added). But the Supreme Court—since the demise of state establishments of religion long ago—has applied that prohibition also to the states and has interpreted it to mean that no governmental entity in the land may sponsor, support, prefer, or inhibit any religion—or all religion.

There is no such restriction upon government with respect to any of the other activities protected by the First Amendment. Conceivably, Congress could set up or subsidize a newspaper, or many of them, to enhance freedom of the press, but it could not set up or subsidize a church. (Government does provide chapels and chaplains for the armed forces and certain hospitals and prisons, but this is not so much "setting up a church" as providing access to churches already existing for those removed by government action from their normal communities.) The same distinction applies to the activities carried on by other public charities or exempt organizations. Some of these contend that they are "given" their exemptions in return for performing public services which government would otherwise have to perform (the doctrine of *quid pro quo*). Private voluntary hospitals are exempt, according to this rationale, because if they did not exist, government would have to build public hospitals to do the work, and in fact has done so in many communities. The same is true of colleges and universities, and (at least potentially) of many other exempt operations. *Except churches.*

Whatever may be the merits of the *quid pro quo* rationale in respect to other non-taxed entities (and from the point of view presented here, it concedes too much in speaking of tax exemption as "given"), it certainly does not apply to churches because the First Amendment forbids the government to set up or operate a church. (In addition— as we shall see later—governments aren't very good at that sort of thing—though they have been trying to set up and sponsor "captive" religions throughout human history.) Of course, the whole *quid pro quo* rationale is unnecessary if one recognizes that most of the non-taxed entities are not part of the wealth-producing engines of revenue anyway. Rather than trying anxiously to "earn" or justify their tax exemption, they should lay the burden of justification on those who would undertake to tax them. (That does not mean they should not pay the costs of municipal services they actually need and use, as we shall see in Chapter 7.)

Whether legislatures do or do not have the power to tax nonprofit voluntary organizations, and particularly public charities[1]—unwise and unprecedented as that would be—it can be argued that, under the First Amendment, they do not have the power—or, more precisely, the *authority,* which is *legitimate* power—to tax *churches.* That was, in fact, the argument presented to the U.S. Supreme Court in the *Walz* case by the National Council of Churches and the Synagogue Council of America in friend-of-the-court briefs. The Supreme Court did not adopt this view, but it did not reject it either. In any event, it is an argument distinguishable from that which can be made by public

1. "Public charities" are almost all Section 501(c)(3) organizations that are not "private foundations" and all Section 170 (b)(1)(A) organizations except those described in Section 170(b)(1)(A)(vii) ("private operating foundations").

charities to which the non-establishment clause of the First Amendment does not apply.

In their own view at least, *churches are not just voluntary nonprofit organizations.* They may *be* that, but they are much more. In duration and extent, they are typically on an entirely different scale from other organizations. A church is part of a vast movement that encompasses millions of adherents in many lands, that has endured for many centuries and will endure for many more. And—the point that will be dealt with at length in the next chapter—the ministrations of churches are not advantageous to their members only but to the society as a whole, and are not merely advantageous to them but crucial for their collective well-being and indeed survival. Unlike other public charities, however meritorious, churches mediate, enable, and fulfill a function that is essential to all known human societies and which government cannot effectively provide. The First Amendment's religion clauses—perhaps intuitively—reflect that claim. It is a sweeping claim, and in the next chapter we will scrutinize it more carefully.

It is for the reason sketched in the preceding paragraph that the interests of churches—in tax matters as in many others—diverge from those of other organizations. That is a hard saying, and there are some who would dispute it, including some church leaders. But the necessity for it should become apparent. Al Hassler, for many years executive director of the Fellowship of Reconciliation, repeatedly made the plea that, with respect to government and the tax code, churches and religious organizations which are not churches should "stick together"—and tactically that is often good advice.

In many areas and for many reasons, the interests of churches and non-ecclesiastical organizations run together. Both may favor (or oppose) abortion or gun control or capital punishment or nuclear power or full employment, and churches can work harmoniously with secular organizations in support of such shared goals, and have often done so. But at some points, particularly having to do with the self-definition, character, and claims of religion, they may be distinct.

To say this is in no way to derogate the importance and value of voluntary organizations—quite the contrary, as spelled out in the preceding chapter—but to say that they are, at some significant points, and at least in the view of churches, very different, for better and worse. That is, in some respects it is advantageous to be a church, in others it is not, such as qualifying for tax subsidies.

Many people may belong to the Fellowship of Reconciliation, for instance, and work through it for the promotion of peace *for religious reasons and in fulfillment of their religious faith.* Some may even find in it their only "religious" outlet or inspiration. But all of that does not make the Fellowship of Reconciliation a *church.* It may hold worship services occasionally, but it does not have a formal, systematic year-round liturgy as its central activity. It has educational programs on peace—and very good ones—but they are not designed to inculcate and nurture the Christian faith *as a whole.* It does not attempt to minister to people in all the successive transitions of life: birth, puberty, marriage, emotional crises, illness, bereavement, and dying. Its members do not consider that they are joining a "church"; many of them already belong to churches to which they look for ministration to their general religious needs. At most, FOR serves or supplements religious interests in a particular sector: the concern for peace. To think of it as a "church" is to misuse the word and to do an injustice to both church and FOR. And the same may be said of other voluntary organizations, however meritorious—and some of them do a better job at what they undertake than some churches do at religion, but it is in no wise the same job.

Religion has its own unique, important—and limited—task or function, and that is not—as commonly supposed—giving off effusions of ingenuous warm amiability in all directions. Let us now examine that function and the conditions which promote and inhibit it.

4

Why Religion Enjoys
a Preferred Position

Religion is entitled to special civil treatment, not just because it deals with the most intense and sensitive commitments of the human heart, but also because it performs a special function in society—one that is of secular importance to everyone—and its special treatment is the best way of insuring that that function is performed. The provisions made in American law for protecting freedom of religion are not just a matter of sentimentally indulging those individuals who are quaintly disposed to such archaic behavior, but a very sensible, hard-headed, present-day way of trying to make available to those who need it, in as many forms and varieties as possible, the crucial ingredient for their lives that religion provides. What is that important function, and how is it best fostered?

The religious believer would immediately reply that what religion furnishes to humankind is *salvation*—or the hope of it—and the best way to foster it would be for everyone immediately to join the particular religion that that believer espouses. That is the True Answer—as seen from *within* any given religion. But it is not necessarily convincing to those *outside,* and it certainly does not persuade them that *they* have a personal stake in fostering that particular religion or all religions. And if they are themselves adherents of another religion, they would have their own True Answer, couched in the terms of that religion. But what society needs for the formulation of civil law to govern everyone is not the True Answer of any one faith, or a set of mutually incompatible True Answers from all faiths, but a pragmatic, proximate answer that does not depend upon acceptance of any one of them, yet is inclusive and considerate of all.

What each religion is doing for its adherents—regardless of what shape "salvation" takes within it, or what Deity or deities it calls upon (if any)—is to help them to "make sense" of life, especially of their own lives, and particularly of those aspects of their lives which are both unsatisfactory and unalterable: failure, handicap, defeat, loss, illness, bereavement, and the prospect of their own death. Those are the experiences that pose most sharply the question of "what is the meaning of life?" and religion tries to provide answers to that question, offering the widest and deepest concepts the human mind can grasp, so that the suffering or perplexed individual can see the pain or difficulty of the moment in a broader perspective of greater good or longer purpose or firmer reality.[1]

Such "explanations" of the ultimate meaning of life may be theistic or non-theistic, naturalistic or supernaturalistic, activistic or quietistic, conventional or bizarre. If they help believers to rise up each morning with hope, to get through the day somehow with purposefulness, and to lie down at night with some sense of satisfaction, they are performing—for *them*—the function of religion, whatever outsiders may think. Not all churches, synagogues, mosques, or temples perform that function well for all believers all the time, and many people may get what ultimate meaning they have from other sources, including some that are not conventionally religious. Yet whatever the source, the function being served is still essentially *religious.*

Not all people feel an equal need at all times for ultimate meaning, and some may go for years—or perchance a lifetime—without experiencing the profound inward pang of desperation to know "what it's all about," "whether I really *matter,*" or "what's the use of it all, anyway?" But for those who do experience it, this threat of meaninglessness can be frightening.[2] Unless most people, most of the time, can

1. For a fuller treatment of the function of religion from this point of view, see the author's *Why Conservative Churches Are Growing* (New York: Harper & Row, 1972), Chapters III and IV.

2. See Peter Berger's description of the nightmare of meaninglessness in *The Sacred Canopy* (Garden City, N.Y.: Doubleday, 1967), pp. 22–27.

find moderately satisfactory ways of answering the ultimate questions
—"Who am I?"/"Why am I here?"/"What is really *real?*"/"What
will be the end of it all?"—the society of which they are a part will
be in peril. Persons who cannot find some kind of more or less satisfy-
ing answers are apt to succumb to despair, bitterness, resentment,
anomie, or to fall into one or another of the escapisms, derangements,
and addictions which are the increasingly prevalent "maladies of
meaninglessness" besetting our society today. Such persons are often
a hazard to themselves and others, sometimes resorting to impulsive
or desperate violence or suicide.

Some people in this plight find a religion which relieves their dis-
tress, others do not. The same mode of "explanation" does not work
for all. Some resonate to a mystic appeal, others to an ascetic one;
some to an otherworldly call, others to a summons to earthly service
to humankind. Fortunately, there are many varieties of religion in our
society, and almost anyone should be able to find one that suits. But
the test of the functional adequacy of a religion is not just in its content
or its initial appeal.

Strange as it may seem, the quality which enables a religion to
satisfy the need for ultimate meaning does not appear to be the co-
gency, reasonableness, plausibility, or even attractiveness as wish-
fulfillment of its doctrinal affirmations, but rather the intensity with
which they are advocated and embodied by a devoted community of
adherents. Intellectual propositions in the abstract do not seem to fill
the hunger for meaning, but rather the continuing, reinforcing experience of a supportive company of fellow believers bound together by
strong commitment to the faith. It is for this reason that there is—
properly speaking—no individual religion, no "instant" religion, no
invisible or disembodied religion. Religion exists as a functioning
reality only to the degree that it is embodied in an ongoing community
—a "church."

That religion will be most *convincing* whose community of faith is
most *serious* about its beliefs.[3] Their seriousness may be manifest in
various ways: by strictness of doctrinal unanimity, by rigor of behavioral or attitudinal conformity, by intensity of emotional investment,

3. This idea is developed at greater length in Chapters V through VIII of the author's
Why Conservative Churches Are Growing.

by depth of commitment of time, energy, money (a relatively "cheap" commodity in religion), and self. There are many ways of carrying out the religious function, each with its own characteristic mode of being serious, and they are not all equally attractive to outsiders who are not at the moment seeking ultimate meaning for their lives. Some emphasize tithing, others faith-healing; some practice foot-washing, others snake-handling; some engage in "speaking in tongues," others in personal evangelizing (probably the most difficult of all). In fact, it may be the very difficulty, "peculiarity," or bizarreness of the religious behavior exhibited that is most compelling in convincing potential converts that "their faith must be true, or they wouldn't *do* such things!"

"Establishment" of Religion

If the function of religion is as important for the survival of society as this analysis suggests, how can society make sure that that function is effectively performed? Historically—and *pre*historically, for that matter—the answer has been for the rulers to favor the functionaries of one or more existing religions with high rank, wealth, power, and other material rewards, while at the same time penalizing or suppressing upstart new religions—the "impious" and "unpatriotic" cults that keep springing up among the "lower orders" of society. Yet somehow these privileges, perquisites, and emoluments (collectively termed the "establishment" of religion) have not insured the effective performance of the religious function—quite the contrary. They have instead contributed to its deterioration. Why should that be?

Let us reflect for a moment on the differential distribution of the goods of this life and the bearing it has on religious behavior. It is one of the plainest and most universal generalizations about human (and even some animal) populations that those traits which cannot be alienated (height, intelligence, etc.) will be distributed "normally" throughout the population. That is, a few people will have a lot, a few will have very little, and most will have a moderate amount, which can be represented graphically by the familiar "bell" curve of a "normal" distribution:

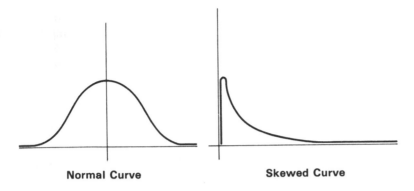

Normal Curve   **Skewed Curve**

On the other hand, those traits which can be alienated—gained or lost
—(weight, wealth, etc.) will be distributed in a "skewed" fashion
among the population, with a few people having a lot and most people
having relatively little. By the very universality of the skewed distribution, one might conjecture that if such traits or attributes were to be
miraculously redistributed so that everyone had an equal amount, it
would not be long—surely not more than six days at the most—until
the skewed distribution would reappear, as a few would have cornered
"the lion's share" again, leaving the rest with little. Perhaps some new
lions would make it to the top of the heap and some old ones not, but
the "heap" would still be there, with most of us not on top of it, but
down toward the bottom somewhere.

Speaking of "heaps," let us tip the skewed distribution up on end,
with the heavy curve downward and the point at the top, forming the
familiar pyramid of social stratification, with the few who are wealthy
and powerful at the top and the many who are poor and weak at the
bottom. This is the Persistent Hierarchical Structure into which human populations arrange themselves (and animal populations too,
where it is called a "pecking order"). It is one of the most pervasive
and intractable realities of human experience. The slope of the pyramid may be steeper or gentler and its floor may be elevated or de-
pressed, but it remains a pyramid, and the outlook and life chances
of each individual will be strongly affected by his or her location in
that structure. One of the most significant dichotomies in human
experience is the line drawn somewhere across the pyramid that di-

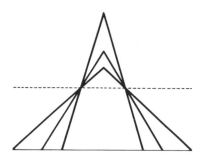

The Persistent Hierarchical Structure

vides the "haves" from the "have-nots." Life looks very different, depending upon whether one is below that line looking up or above it looking down. Religion looks very different too.

Religious movements begin, as a rule, among the "have-nots" and have their greatest impact there, perhaps because the "have-nots" know a disproportionate share of miserable yet unavoidable experiences. Having less in the way of material resources to shield themselves from adversity, they have a more acute and continuous need to "make sense" of their lives. To say that they have a greater and more intense "need" for religion than the "haves" does not mean that the "haves" possess it and they do not. On the contrary, the "have-nots" are often more fervent and winsome adherents of religion than the "haves." Actually, among the "have-nots" there are fewer individuals in proportion who are religious adherents, but their involvement with religion is more intense than is that of the "haves," among whom a much larger proportion have a veneer of religion, while few have as intense an attachment to it. Religion is for the "haves" more a habitual aspect of their status *persona,* an attribute of their attained position of respectability.

This contrast comes about in part because an effectively functioning religion helps its adherents to cope with their life-situations, to bounce back from difficulties with resilience and confidence restored. Often a by-product of religion's stabilizing effect is that its adherents rise in the socio-economic scale and become "haves" themselves. In the process, they gradually come to feel a less intense attachment for religion; it becomes a more routinized part of their lives and makes more modest demands upon their time and effort. This process was visible in the early Wesleyan Revival in England, causing its founder, John Wesley, to observe:

> Wherever riches have increased, the essence of religion has decreased in the same proportion. Therefore, I do not see how it is possible, in the nature of things, for any revival of religion to continue long. For religion must necessarily produce both industry and frugality, and these cannot but produce riches. But as riches increase, so will pride, anger, and love of the world in all its branches. . . . Is there no way to prevent this—this continued decay of pure religion?[4]

In the upward transition, the adherents' religion undergoes changes too; it becomes more relaxed, more restrained, more decorous, more "respectable." It ceases to be as strident, as "fanatical," as disruptive, as denunciatory of the Way Things Are; it has been domesticated to fit in with its adherents' new outlook, which has become more accepting of a world in which they have found their social bearings. Religion and adherents have pulled themselves up through the great barrier; they have "made the grade"; they no longer see things with the same eyes—or even speak the same language—as the "have-nots." And the "have-nots" must turn to another religion or a new religion—or more usually to a new form of the old "ascended" religion—to find the help they need: a religion that expresses *their* condition, that is not so solicitous of the "haves" and the way they run the world to benefit themselves.

One significant difference between the religion of the "haves" and the "have-nots" may be the latter's apocalypticism—the belief that the present world is evil and will be destroyed catastrophically by the power of God, whereupon the righteous poor will be exalted. The "haves" don't think that way! They prefer something a little more like the "Deuteronomic Formula": prosperity is the reward of piety (or virtue), whereas suffering is the consequence of sin. It is interesting to note the traces of "have-not" religion still visible in early strata of the New Testament; compare the "have-not" version of the Beatitudes in Luke 6:20–26:

4. Quoted in Max Weber, *The Protestant Ethic and the Spirit of Capitalism* (New York: Charles Scribner's Sons, 1930), p. 175.

Blessed are *you* poor, for yours is the kingdom of God.
Blessed are *you* that hunger now, for you shall be satisfied.
Blessed are *you* that weep now, for you shall laugh. . . .

But woe to you that are rich, for you have received your consolation.
Woe to you that are full now, for you shall hunger.
Woe to you that laugh now, for you shall mourn and weep.

with the "haves' " "spiritualized" version in Matthew 5:3–11:

Blessed are the poor *in spirit,* for theirs is the
   kingdom of heaven. . . .
Blessed are the meek, for they shall inherit the earth.
Blessed are those who hunger and thirst *for righteousness,*
   for they shall be satisfied. (emphasis added)

There are other wisps of "have-not" religion showing through in the story of Dives and Lazarus (the rich man whose role in the afterlife was reversed with that of the poor man who had lain at his gate, Luke 16:19–31), the letter of James ("Come now, you rich, weep and howl for the miseries that are coming upon you," James 5:1–6 as well as 2:1–7, "Is it not the rich who oppress you, is it not they who drag you into court?"), and in the Magnificat (Luke 1:46–55). Halford Luccock relates that, when that great hymn of the Nativity was chanted at Christmas in the crowded medieval Cathedral of Paris, at a certain point there came such a triumphant roar from the poor people in the nave that the ceremony was interrupted until order was restored; the words that inspired such uproar were: "He has put down the mighty from their thrones, and exalted those of low degree; he has filled the hungry with good things, and the rich he has sent empty away." This seemed like such an excellent program to "those of low degree" that they couldn't contain themselves and had to shout their approval. Needless to say, the "haves" didn't see anything to cheer about in those sentiments. By and large, they have found ways to eradicate or reinterpret most of those disquieting early passages.

From this one particular religious tradition we can gain a sense of the distinction between the kind of religion that appeals to the "haves" as contrasted with the kind that appeals to the "have-nots." The reason for this venture into a comparison of religious doctrines is to show why "establishment" of religion doesn't work. The people who arrange the "establishment" and whose religion is the one to be favored with privileges and benefits, prestige and the official sponsorship of the state are, of course, the "haves." Their religion is not only unusable to the "have-nots"—the people who need the function of religion most—because it doesn't "explain" *their* lives, but the very act of "establishing" it as official and respectable and "required" makes it part of the problem that needs to be "explained."

In addition, the "established" religion loses much of its persuasiveness even among the "haves," since the quality that makes it convincing is its *cost* to the believer, and the effect of "establishment" is precisely to take the cost out of religion. The favored religion no longer requires the degree of exertion, sacrifice, endurance of persecution that once gave it preciousness to the believer—or any degree at all. It doesn't even require mild nonconformity any more, since it has become the Accepted Thing to Do.

As the "established" religion prospers, its functionaries demonstrate the paradox first pointed out by C. Northcote Parkinson ("Parkinson's Paradox") with respect to governmental occupations: the *more secure their situations, the less productive they become.*[5] They come to feel that their stipends and emoluments are given in recognition of their *being* rather than their *doing.* They tend to wax fat and indolent. They neglect their duties, or delegate them to apprentices and underlings. Under these circumstances, it is not surprising that the religion these functionaries serve begins to lose adherents, actual and potential, to competing religious bodies whose diligence and zeal have not (yet) suffered the debilitating rewards of official favor—the new cults of the "have-nots"!

The response of the "establishment" to such competition from below is seldom increased vigor and productivity. Instead, the effort is invariably made to suppress the competition, and the heavy hand of the state is called into play to protect the favored faith from "unworthy" rivals. Persecution follows, the devotion of the non-established groups is stimulated by danger, the cost of adherence among them is increased—and with it the convincingness of their

5. Paraphrased from *Parkinson's Law* (Boston: Houghton Mifflin, 1957).

beliefs—while the "establishment" is debased by having had to call in the state to defend it. The suppression of one religion by or for the benefit of another is a common but ugly course of events, by which none of the participants is improved. The suppressed religion's adherents are, of course, discouraged and embittered, though some may also become more determined and devoted to their ostensibly discredited faith. The state has made critics and enemies at home and often abroad, including some who might have become its staunchest citizens as they worked their way up in the world. And the "established" religion is not invigorated but rather confirmed in its pretensions and sinks further into that characteristic blend of arrogance and debility that "establishment" fosters.

As we look back across the centuries, we can see countless such grim and grisly episodes: the orthodox crusades against the Cathari and the Waldensians, the hounding of the Anabaptists from country to country, the massacre of the Huguenots on St. Bartholomew's Day, the burning of Michael Servetus in Calvin's Geneva, the hanging of Quaker Mary Dyer on Boston Common, the slaughter of Catholics by Protestants and of Protestants by Catholics (unto this very day in Ulster) and of Jews by both. It is hard to avoid the conclusion that religious conflict can stir up and release some of the fiercest and most unforgiving animosities known to history. Because religion is such a deep and intense and elemental part of human life, it can be dangerous when threatened, and for this reason conflict is perhaps more characteristic of religion—particularly of vital religion—than is "sweetness and light."

Force is of little avail in trying to spread religion or to stop its spread, and often generates virulent resistance and resentment. After centuries of bitter trial and error, some governments have wisely come to the conclusion that the best way to handle the problem of religion is to *leave it alone,* neither preferring nor suppressing. The founders of the United States took this view—among the first in the world to do so—and made admirably gingerly provisions for the carrying on of the religious function without governmental "help" or hindrance, without even the appearance of governmental sponsorship, favoritism, entanglement, or duress. Sometimes those provisions appear to *benefit* the religious enterprise more than others (as by chaplaincies or tax exemptions); sometimes they seem to *disfavor* them (as by denial of tax support or subsidy). But their overall effect is to maximize the possibility of the fulfillment of the religious function in the only way government can—by leaving it strictly "on its own"—which is precisely the arrangement commanded by the two religion clauses of the First Amendment.

Thus each religion is left free to "sink or swim" in reliance upon its ability to attract and retain adherents, presumably by virtue of its ability to perform for them the function it claims to be able to perform —religion. Tax exemption is of the very essence of that relationship between government and religion: it neither gives to the organizations of religion anything they would not otherwise have nor takes away from them anything they have attracted from adherents on their own merits, and the same applies equally to all religious groups.

The next question, then, is *who qualifies* for this preferred position?

5

Who Qualifies for the Preferred Position?

For whatever reasons, religion *is* accorded a "preferred position" in American law. But who qualifies for that position? And—equally important—who determines who qualifies? Even if the exposition in the preceding chapters be granted, there remains a series of difficult "boundary" and "gatekeeper" questions to be resolved.

Since the law is enacted, administered, and interpreted by various branches of government, it is necessarily government which determines who qualifies under the law's various terms. The government is the "gatekeeper." With respect to religion, this function of government poses some problems. The question becomes not *whether* the government shall keep the gate, but *how* it does so. Is it the responsibility of government to define what constitutes "religion" or a "church"? Or should religious bodies themselves define what "religion" is? But would that not be a unilateral and self-serving sort of definition such as no other entity referred to in the law can fashion for itself?

The hazards of government definition of religion are great. Among them is the temptation to define religion in ways that are essentially supportive of government itself or of the status quo. Then those organizations would qualify for tax exemption which do not "rock the boat" or criticize governmental leadership. Such an arrangement would be a form of the *quid pro quo* type of bargain referred to earlier, in which churches are supposedly "given" tax exemption in return for certain services or in recognition of certain merits—*to be determined by government.* This sort of "trade" or preferential selectivity on the part of government is the essence of "establishment of religion," since it opens the gate to some and closes it to others on the basis of "political" criteria extraneous to the performance of the religious function, favoring docile and domesticated applicants and rejecting "radical" and "subversive" ones.

The greater problem with such governmental favoritism, however, is that it usually favors the "wrong" churches. That is, the churches most valuable for the survival of society are those which are most effectively fulfilling the function of religion. But they are often not the churches which appear most attractive to government. (The same phenomenon is seen in other realms, such as the press, where those newspapers, broadcasters, and reporters most effectively serving the people's need and right to know what government is doing are often the ones posing the greatest threat to the security of governmental incumbents.)

The ironic paradox that government is prone to prefer the "wrong" churches is nowhere more evident than in the present situation, in which certain large "mainline" ecumenical and ethically oriented denominations have consciously undertaken by service and social action to improve the plight of the disadvantaged. These are the kinds of churches that—so long as they do not succeed in bringing about any real changes (as, by and large, they have not)—would be most acceptable to government. They are respectable, decorous, circumspect, predictable, and do not really muster enough lay advocacy on behalf of the poor to threaten anyone. But they are not the churches that appeal to the poor!

When the poor need religious help, where do they go? To the non-"respectable," unconventional, "lowbrow," radical, and bizarre religions—Jehovah's Witnesses, Black Muslims, speaking-in-tongues Pentecostals, storefront fundamentalist Tabernacles, independent "Bible-believing" Baptist temples, etc.—"upstart" cults of the "lower orders" which government would be less likely to recognize as "legitimate" religions. Yet these are the very churches that are best performing the function of religion—explaining the ultimate meaning of life —to the people who need it most and whom the "mainline" denominations seem unable to reach (perhaps for reasons spelled out under the heading of "establishment" in the preceding chapter).

It is precisely because government will not be able or willing to recognize those churches[1] that are most effectively performing the function of religion where it is most needed that government must not be responsible for picking and choosing among churches (and would-be churches) on the basis of its own ("political") preferences and predilections. That way "establishment" lies.

The government's responsibility as "gatekeeper" is a much narrower one. It is not to sort out "legitimate" religions or churches from those that are not, or respectable from "fanatical," or "responsible" from "radical," or conventional from innovative, but simply to admit to the "preferred position" any organization engaged in the practice of *religion*. The sole applicable criterion is simple enough to state, according to the rationale set forth here: *any organization performing the function of religion—explaining the ultimate meaning of life for its adherents—is entitled to the status of "church," and those which do not, are not.* But how is that criterion to be applied? It may not be readily apparent from a brief, external inspection which is which—though a group like the "Universal Life Church," which has *no* doctrines or tenets, can hardly be offering *any* explanation of the meaning of life.

Certain facets of this principle should be pointed out:

(1) To qualify, a group must *claim* to be a "church," or to be engaged in religion (not just in "religious activities" but in carrying on, promulgating, practicing, and perpetuating a religion as a whole).

(2) That religion may take any form and have any content imaginable, so long as it *offers some explanation of the ultimate meaning of life,* i.e., the nature, duty, purpose and/or destiny of humankind. It may or may not be "theistic." It may or may not believe in a "supernatural" world. It may or may not have ethical precepts or implications. It may or may not have specially trained full-time professional leaders or "clergy."

1. For example, Black Muslims have repeatedly been characterized as a "political" movement by wardens of prisons, police chiefs, mayors, and other governmental agencies. In recent years, however, most courts have recognized that the Black Muslims are a "religion" protected by the First Amendment.

WHO QUALIFIES FOR THE PREFERRED POSITION?   61

(3) That church will have a *body of adherents* with sufficient *continuity* to be identifiable over time and sufficient *numbers* to support it by their voluntary contributions. That is, it must have some corporate existence (not in the sense of being incorporated, but a collectivity, a body) and be economically self-sufficient.

The problem of defining "church" and "religion" has perplexed administrative agencies and courts for a long time. One of the early problems to be posed was a nontheistic religion, and the U.S. Circuit Court of Appeals for the District of Columbia Circuit concluded that the Washington Ethical Society could not be denied tax exemption merely because it did not worship a deity.[2] A similar result was reached by the Court of Appeals of California in the same year (1957), which went on to say:

> The only way the state can determine the existence or nonexistence of "religious worship" is to approach the problem objectively. It is not permitted to test validity of, or to compare beliefs. This simply means that "religion" fills a void that exists in the lives of most men. Regardless of why a particular belief suffices, as long as it serves this purpose, it must be accorded the same status of an orthodox religious belief. . . . Religion simply includes: (1) a belief, not necessarily referring to supernatural powers; (2) a cult, involving a gregarious association openly expressing the belief; (3) a system of moral practice directly resulting from an adherence to the belief; and (4) an organization within the cult designed to observe the tenets of belief. The content of the belief is of no moment. Assuming this definition of "religion" is correct, then it necessarily follows that any lawful means of formally observing the tenets of the cult is "worship," within the meaning of the tax-exemption provision.[3]

This influential decision, which foreshadowed more visible ones,[4] attempts to characterize religion functionally, structurally, or operationally rather than by defining its "content," though the terms "cult," "association," "organization," "belief," "tenets," and "worship" seem to revolve around one another in a rather circular fashion.

2. 249 F.2d 127 (1957).
3. *Fellowship of Humanity* v. *Alameda County,* 153 C.A. 2d at 692–3 (1957).
4. *Torcaso* v. *Watkins,* 367 U.S. 488 (1962); *U.S.* v. *Seeger,* 380 U.S. 163 (1964).

But perhaps it indicates a receptivity in the courts to the mode of thinking set forth here.

Congress and the U.S. Supreme Court, however, over a period of two hundred years have never found it necessary to define "religion" or "church." The Treasury, in developing regulations to implement the Internal Revenue Code, experimented with an interesting tack. It did not attempt to define a "church," but it proposed a definition of the next nearest entity, a religious organization which, though not itself a church, qualifies for deductibility of contributions under Section 170(b)(1)(A)(i), which refers to "a church or a convention or association of churches":

> ... the term "church" includes a religious order or a religious organization if such order or organization:
>
> (1) Is an integral part of a church, and
>
> (2) Is engaged primarily in carrying out the religious functions of a church. . . . In determining whether a religious order or organization is an integral part of a church . . . , consideration will be given to the degree to which it is connected with, and controlled by, such church. In determining whether a religious order or organization is engaged primarily in carrying out the religious functions of a church . . . , the principal consideration will be whether the duties of such order or organization include the ministration of sacerdotal functions and the conduct of religious worship.[5]

In hearings on this proposed regulation, the U.S. Catholic Conference took the view that the government's definition was appropriate but inadequate, and offered what it believed to be a more comprehensive one:

> An organization is a church or convention or association of churches . . . if the conduct of religious worship, religious preaching, or the administration incidental thereto, is one of its primary purposes and substantial operations. For purposes of this paragraph, "religious worship" includes all forms of liturgy, including prayer and meditation services and the conduct of such religious rites as baptism, marriage, ordination and burial. "Religious preaching" includes religious education in all its forms.

5. Proposed Treasury Regulation Section 1.170A-9(a), 36 *Federal Register* 9298, May 22, 1971.

The National Council of Churches, in its comments on the regulation, praised the Treasury for not attempting to define "church," and suggested that "religious organization" could be defined by use of other terms already in the Code:

> The term "church" includes religious orders and any other organization which. . . . (1) Is an integral part of, or is controlled by or closely connected with, a church or convention or association of churches, and (2) Is engaged primarily in carrying out the religious purposes of such church or convention or association of churches.

The regulation that elicited all of this commentary has never been finalized and promulgated by the Treasury.

More recently, the Treasury tried another tack in attempting to pin down the general locus of churches.[6] This time it focused on another peripheral category: not churches themselves, but "their integrated auxiliaries"—a term found in Section 6033(a)(2)(A)(i), exempting the described entities from the obligation to file annual informational returns (Form 990) with the Internal Revenue Service.

This, too, was unacceptable to many religious bodies, which filed vehement objections. The term "integrated auxiliaries" is not used by any religious body in this country to refer to any of its parts or subsidiaries. Senator Wallace Bennett (R-Utah) had suggested the term "auxiliaries" during Finance Committee consideration of that section of the Code, using a term familiar to his own (Mormon) church to refer to the men's or women's organizations of a church, or its youth groups. But this term seemed a bit loose to Treasury, which persuaded the Committee to introduce the modifier "integrated" before it, producing a strange hybrid unknown to any existing ecclesiastical nomenclature. (See note at end of chapter.)

The churches, by and large, have been very resistant to government's defining what a "church" is or what "religion" is—and rightly so. They have maintained that "religion" is what churches *do,* and that everyone *knows* what "churches" are, since they were here, engaged in *religion,* long before there ever was a United States of America! New entries in the field can be recognized by whether they are derived from, or resemble, existing ones. But

6. Proposed Treasury Regulation Section 1.6033–2, 41 *Federal Register* 6073, February 11, 1976.

what does it mean to "resemble" existing churches? How close must the resemblance be?

Some courts have recently felt obliged to rule that various organizations are "religions" or "churches" because they *claimed* to be: The Church of Scientology, the Church of the New Song, the Process Church of the Final Judgment, the Universal Life Church, etc. Some of these are viewed by long-recognized churches as deliberate imposters—which they may be, but how is the secular magistrate to determine that in the absence of clear evidence of insincerity or fraud?[7] By asking existing churches? They are perhaps the least likely to recognize in an upstart competitor the legitimacy of new forms of the religious enterprise.

Should the magistrate consult respected scholars in the "scientific" study of the sociology of religion? They do not necessarily agree among themselves on what "religion" is, let alone on whether a particular organization is entitled to call itself a "church." And even if they did agree, would that be determinative? Would it not still be an "outsider's" verdict? How can anyone assess from "outside" whether a given would-be "church" is meeting its members' religious needs? Only the members themselves can testify to that, and they do it most plainly by continuing to belong, or not continuing.

Yet the magistrate, by the very nature of the secular judicial function, must make an outsider's judgment, without entanglement in the internal affairs of religion. On what basis can that judgment be made? Someone must decide whether a group qualifies under the law as a "church"—for purposes of reporting, for example. Do they get it, or don't they? The magistrate does not have the luxury of being able to avoid the question. In this unenviable position, magistrates have often erred in either of two opposite ways: by being overanxious not to be hoodwinked by charlatans posing as leaders of a "religion," or by being in too great haste to assess—and accept—the bona fides of newcomers to the field of religion. Both of these errors are tragic—and unnecessary.

Charlatanry in religion is neither as prevalent nor as pernicious as some magistrates seem to feel. People are entitled to let themselves be fooled if they want to. The authors of the First Amendment were

7. Cf. *U.S.* v. *Ballard* (322 U.S. 78 (1944)), where the Court held that a jury could not assess the truth or falsity of religious claims, but could assess their sincerity.

willing to take a calculated risk of tolerating occasional religious charlatans rather than giving the government the responsibility of investigating, supervising, and—in consequence—sponsoring and controlling, the practitioners of religion. It should not be the responsibility of government to inspect and certify religions as it does meat. Consumers of religion will need to be their own guardians to a greater degree than in other areas of consumership not protected by the First Amendment: that is the meaning of *freedom,* and particularly of *religious* freedom. (This question will be treated also with respect to regulation of charitable solicitations, Chapter 8, and under the topic of limitations on religious liberty in Chapter 7.)

On the other hand, *new* religions *do* emerge from time to time, and should not be disadvantaged by their dissimilarities from existing religions. The Black Muslims, for instance, are unconventional in many ways and have given expression to many abrasive views and emotions, yet the movement has also been able to transform the lives of thousands of black people, including criminals, alcoholics, and drug addicts, whom no other religious groups seemed able to reach.[8] If any group is entitled to the "preferred position" accorded religion, the Black Muslims are.

Fortunately, it is not necessary for the magistrate to make either of these errors. There is a simple, objective, external test which can be applied without entanglement to determine the bona fides of groups claiming to be churches. It is the *test of time.*

Religious movements exist on a scale measured in centuries, with lifespans in which the passage of a decade is but the winking of an eye. No one should have to judge whether a claimant group is a "religion" or a "church" on the basis of a few months' or a few years' evidence. Until it has survived the various crises, doldrums, tensions, and attritions that beset all organizational beginnings, the group is still an infant, and it does not yet appear what it shall be.

A religion doesn't become *visible* as such until it is shared by a committed group of people and has lasted at least a couple of generations. Until then, it is not so much a religion as a proposal for one. Whether the proposal is accepted . . . remains to be seen.[9]

8. Kelley, *Why Conservative Churches are Growing,* pp. 168-9.
9. *Ibid.,* pp. 44-45.

The magistrate can and should say to the new[10] organization applying for tax exemption: "You are entitled to tax exemption as a non-profit voluntary organization with religious purposes, as provided by Section 501(c)(3) of the Internal Revenue Code. Whether you are also a *church* cannot be determined at this time. Come back in twenty (or thirty, or fifty) years and we will see. Meanwhile, you have the full freedom of speech, press, and assembly that churches (and other organizations) have, and if your claims to be a church are validated by your adherents' continuing support for that period, there is no basis on which your claims can then be denied."

The applicant might contend that the equal protection of the laws (guaranteed by the Fourteenth Amendment) applies to *new* religions as well as *old,* and the magistrate would reply, "Certainly it does, and as soon as you have been in existence for twenty years, you will begin to qualify as a new religion. Until that time, you are an *invitation* to religion that is still being considered." The law recognizes many time-conditioned categories: attaining majority, establishing residence, presumption of death, recognition of a common-law marriage, etc. There is no reason that such an elementary and reasonable condition should not also apply to qualifying as a religion or a church. The actual threshold is a subject for negotiation: fifty years may be too long; ten years is certainly the bare minimum; it is the principle that is urged here, not a specific period of time.

At the expiration of the specified period of time, any group claiming throughout that period to be a religion or church and supporting itself continuously by voluntary contributions on the basis of that claim would be automatically accorded the status claimed. Beyond inspecting its claims and longevity, the magistrate would have nothing further to do with it. Thus the actual decision would be made, not by the magistrate from "outside," but by the members within. Only if *they* found sufficient merit in the group's work as a church to support it and to continue supporting it for twenty years, would it qualify as a church. If they did not so support it, it would not qualify. If they did so support it as meeting their religious needs (whether or not those needs or the way they are met are as described in this book), on what

10. This would not apply, of course, to existing churches, schismatic groups breaking off from existing churches, or mergers of existing churches.

basis could the magistrate determine that they were not entitled to be a church?

Some would immediately raise the questions of fraud or duress. The fraud in question would not be fraud by the leader(s) upon the members, which—certainly over a period of twenty years—they are best able to detect, but fraud by leader(s) and members together upon the magistrate. That is, if both leader(s) and members had conspired together to represent as a "church" what was really a commercial business, a drug ring, a gambling club, or a brothel (as actually happened in one instance in Nevada), then the application would be void. But twenty years is a long time to carry on a continuous deception involving enough people to give credence to the claim of voluntary support. And in the interim, the applicant organization would be obliged to file annual informational returns about its leadership, financing, and operations (under Section 6033 of the Internal Revenue Code) which should give some evidence of whether its activities are as they are claimed to be.

"Duress" would be a condition in which the members of the group are compelled to support it, or to pretend to support it, through blackmail, intimidation, or other coercive means, which would not only void the application for recognition as a church but might also lead to criminal prosecution. Various groups have been accused recently of holding members in "captivity" by means of "brainwashing," hypnosis, or drugs, but thus far these remain mere allegations —typical "outsider's" denunciations of religious behavior they do not share or understand. Of course, if any group *is* using such techniques, the case should be proven by evidence, and if proven in a court of law, they should be punished severly for violating one of the most vital and sensitive rights in human society. But so far there has been no such case; just allegations.

Suppose a new prophet or messiah should arise—as one does almost every day—proclaiming the most bizarre of nonsense—as most do, at least in the estimation of outsiders—and practicing peculiar rites and regimens—as they invariably appear to people accustomed to practices that were equally outlandish when first introduced. A few devotees may be attracted for a while by the very novelty of the performance, and this new prophet or messiah may enjoy a brief popularity while he or she is the current fad among aficionados of religious prodigies.

But mere spectacularity or sensationalism alone cannot keep a religious movement going for very long. It usually takes tremendous energy, zeal, persistence, and hard work to get a religious movement "off the ground" and to keep it going. Those of us who have been involved in leading a local congregation can testify that it is no easy task. Anyone contemplating setting up any voluntary organization, let alone a church or even a pseudo-church, and keeping it going just to qualify for tax exemption would find it easier to pay taxes!

If this putative prophet or messiah can keep people coming back for more, year after year, for twenty years, despite disputes and disappointments, defections and adversities, he or she is evidently providing something that they need. Whatever outsiders may think, he or she is not a charlatan but a practitioner of *religion,* entitled to all of the (rather limited) privileges and immunities thereof. Anyone able to "hoodwink" a following for that long is also providing them with some kind of understanding of the ultimate meaning of life (conceivably, even if he doesn't believe it himself). On what ground, then, could one say that he or she is not entitled to the status of "church"? Rejection by the local Ministerial Association? As suggested earlier, apprehensive rivals are not the best judges of unconventional practitioners of religion, any more than physicians as a group are of chiropractic or acupuncture.

During the twenty or so years of "probation," the would-be religious organization is exempt from taxation but subject to whatever requirements of registration, reporting, disclosure, audit, and examination apply to other nonprofit voluntary organizations. After qualifying as an authentic "church," however, it is no longer subject to governmental examination, investigation, regulation—or support. It is in a "preferred position," to be sure, but not a very luxurious one.

No class of persons or organizations should enjoy a special status under the law unless there is justification for it based upon, not just the interests of the particular beneficiaries, but the interests of the whole society. Such a justification has been attempted here. If there is no such justification, then tax exemption and other legal prerogatives and immunities are indeed special privileges in the worst sense.

That there is a secular justification for such public policy does not make it a *quid pro quo,* a "service" which churches must render or lose their tax exemption, because government is not able to determine whether a given church is actually fulfilling the function of religion or not. Only its members can determine that. As long as they continue to support it, government has no right under the First Amendment to interfere. When they decline to support it, government has no right to keep it going. It will cease to exist, and whether it is tax-exempt or not will make little difference then.[11]

11. On January 4, 1977, the *Federal Register* carried the final version of a Treasury regulation defining "integrated auxiliary" of a church, as used in Section 6033(a)(2)(A)(i), exempting certain organizations from the requirement of filing annual informational returns. It states, in effect, that if an organization claiming to be an "integrated auxiliary" of a church would have been classified as "educational" or "charitable" rather than exclusively "religious" if applying for its own exemption, it is not an "integrated auxiliary" of a church. If it is "exclusively religious" and is controlled by or associated with a church, it may qualify as an "integrated auxiliary" and be exempted from filing informational returns.

Parochial schools are excused from filing such returns under the Secretary's discretionary authority. So are organizations that do not have a "separate legal identity" from the church of which they are a part. The main effect of this regulation seems to be to require all separately incorporated hospitals, colleges, orphanages, etc., to file annual informational returns, whether they are related to a church or not. Churches are not pleased that the Internal Revenue Service will still try to define what is "exclusively religious" in organizations related to churches.

6

Must Churches Be Silent to Qualify?

Since the beginning of the nation, churches (and other non-wealth-producing organizations) have not been expected or required to share their income (at least that income consisting of voluntary contributions from adherents) with government—an arrangement generally but somewhat inaccurately referred to as "tax exemption." As noted earlier, this is a salutary arrangement that has helped to nurture the development of diverse centers of citizen initiative so essential to the flourishing of democracy.

But in 1934 a curious curtailment was introduced into that arrangement—one which has since expanded and rigidified to a degree alarming to its victims and not intended by its originators. In that year, Congress was considering revisions of the Internal Revenue Code, among which was an addition to what is now Section 501(c)(3). The Senate Finance Committee seems to have had in mind excluding from that category "sham" organizations that were really a "front" for lobbying on behalf of wealthy donors' private interests. As Senator Harrison, floor manager for the bill, remarked:

> I may say to the Senate that the attention of the Senate Committee was called to the fact that there are certain organizations which are receiving contributions in order to influence legislation and carry on propaganda. The committee thought there ought to be an amendment that would stop that, so that is why we have put this amendment in the bill.[1]

1. 78 Congressional Record 5959 (1934).

Senator Reed of Pennsylvania, a member of the Committee, noted that the amendment was a bit broader than the Committee's intention, but did not suggest any better wording:

> As that amendment is worded, it would apply to the Society for the Prevention of Cruelty to Children, to the Society for the Prevention of Cruelty to Animals, *or any of the worthy institutions that we do not in the slightest mean to affect.* . . . There is no reason why a contribution . . . should be deductible as if it were a charitable contribution if it is a selfish one made to advance the personal interests of the giver of the money. That is what the committee were trying to reach; but we found great difficulty in phrasing the amendment. I do not reproach the draftsmen. I think we gave them an impossible task; but this amendment goes much further than the committee intended to go.[2]

Nevertheless, it was adopted, and reads as follows:

> . . . no substantial part of the activities of which is carrying on propaganda, or otherwise attempting, to influence legislation.

It was also inserted in other sections of the Internal Revenue Code, such as that describing organizations to which contributions can be given that donors may deduct from their taxable income (Section 170(c)(2)(D)). It is often referred to as the "lobbying" limitation, and it started a trend of thinking that became increasingly popular in Congress, so that twenty years later there rose up another Senator, Lyndon B. Johnson, to add a similar limitation in similarly tortured prose, this one prohibiting "electioneering":

> . . . and which does not participate in, or intervene in (including the publishing or distribution of statements), any political campaign on behalf of any candidate for public office.

It is interesting to note that the ban on lobbying leaves a margin for insubstantial activity, but the ban on electioneering is absolute. Curiously, no one knows what the word "substantial" means in this context. It is not defined in Treasury regulations spelling out the effect of this section, nor is there any ruling by the Internal Revenue Service to guide public charities in knowing whether their activities

2. 78 Congressional Record 5861 (1934). Emphasis added.

in regard to legislation are "substantial" or not.

There is one court decision to the effect that an organization which expended 5% of its annual budget on lobbying was *not* engaged to a "substantial" degree,[3] and this figure of 5% has been widely supposed to be a magic number or "rule-of-thumb" employed by the Internal Revenue Service, but there is no written evidence that such is the case, nor even that the test of substantiality is a proportionate one or refers to expenditures. In fact, another court has used words that do not imply arithmetical considerations at all. It was enough for that court that an organization's legislative activities were an "essential" part of its program, that they were not "incidental" but "substantial and continuous."[4] (Perhaps the sharpest test would be whether the legislative efforts of an organization— however minimal—were *successful.*)

The undefined word "substantial" thus stands as an enigmatic threat to any public charity contemplating action on any legislative issue, and often has the "chilling effect" of persuading it that the only really safe course is to refrain from such activity entirely. It serves to muzzle, immobilize, or emasculate public charities with respect to affecting public policy, even though their charitable purposes may be fully effectuated only by obtaining changes in public policy and, more importantly, the public dialogue may be impoverished without their free participation. The very fact that an organization's purposes can be fully effectuated only by changes in public policy has been deemed by the Internal Revenue Service to disqualify it for Section 501(c)(3) status and to categorize it as an "action organization"—Section 501(c)(4). It was on that basis that Americans United for Separation of Church and State lost its exemption (deductibility).

Voluntary organizations have a wealth of information and experience to contribute to the public dialogue that would be of great help to governmental policy-makers in the fields of health, education, social welfare, environmental conservation, consumer protection, and many others. Yet, because of the fear of losing deductibility, many of these organizations are very wary about doing anything that might be

3. *Seasongood* v. *Commissioner,* 227 F.2d 907 (6th Cir. 1955). See Appendix A.
4. *Christian Echoes National Ministry, Inc.* v. *U.S.,* 470 F.2d 849 (1972).

perceived as "lobbying." Some are totally inhibited on this score, sometimes intimidated by the ominous warnings of conservatives on their boards, who play upon the fears of the less well-informed by conjuring up visions of the organization's losing its tax exemption if it takes a contemplated action pertaining to an issue that might at some time become a subject of legislation. Thus the vague and undefined word "substantial" has become a weapon in the hands of those who wish to keep the public charities quiescent—which may be precisely what some legislators want.

It is certainly apparent that many members of Congress have found the tax laws a useful device for limiting citizen intrusions into the realm of legislation. Not only was the stricture on "lobbying" followed by one on "electioneering," but both were reinforced by restrictions in the Tax Reform Act of 1969 on private foundations—a new category created by that Act—prohibiting them from supporting voter registration drives confined to a single election or carried on in fewer than five states (Section 4945). Counter-pressures in Congress did succeed in eliminating certain activities from the statutory definition of "influencing legislation":

—making available the results of nonpartisan analysis, study or research; (Section 4945(e))
—appearances before, or communications to, any legislative body with respect to a possible decision of such body which might affect the existence of the organization, its powers and duties, its tax-exempt status, or the deduction of contributions to it; (Section 4945(e))
—providing technical advice or assistance to a governmental body in response to a written request from that body; (Section 4945(e)(2))

But the prevailing sentiment in Congress seems to be an increasing disposition to make it harder, not easier, for citizens to communicate their views effectively to the persons they elect and pay to make the laws under which they live. As noted in Chapter 1, Congress eased the path for businesses in 1962 by amending Section 162(e) to permit them to deduct the costs of influencing legislation affecting their direct interests, while denying such deductibility for contributions by citizens to charitable organizations seeking to influence legislation in the *public* interest.

This disposition was elegantly expressed by one Congressperson who explained to a group of church people that his colleagues felt more at ease with the interventions of "professional lobbyists" who took care to "preserve their access" to legislators than they did with "amateurs" often interested only in "single-issue politics." What this means is that the good members would like to avoid the full rigors of the democratic process if possible. They would rather not be accosted by real, live, individual voters or their spokesmen, who are concerned not just about making money for themselves but about the good of the whole nation (as they see it). The members feel more comfortable with the smooth, obsequious, well-heeled emissaries of Boeing, ITT, or Gulf & Western than they do with the putative hordes of hot-eyed fanatics descending upon them with unseemly threats and demands. The latter is a supposed peril which Congress, since the happy discovery of the 1934 lobbying limitation, has taken increasing care to keep at a safe distance by erecting barriers to it in the tax code.

It is sometimes argued in defense of this Congressional trend that the members have no aversion to meeting individual voters from their own districts. What they don't want is to have political pressures focused upon them from other parts of the nation by national organizations which would want to retain full-time lobbyists in the capital with tax-deductible funds. But is there not an element of ingenuousness in this defense? After all, members of Congress affect the lives of people all over the country by their decisions, particularly if they are ranking members of important committees, and it should be possible for the people whose lives are being affected to communicate their wishes and concerns to those making the decisions.

Furthermore, it is a dangerous romanticism to insist that only individual citizens in dispersion have the right to "attempt to influence legislation." As de Tocqueville observed long ago, in a situation of general equality, individuals have little effect unless they can "combine"—join themselves together and act in concert to advance their interests. To require citizens to act solely as individuals in the public arena is to condemn them to perpetual futility. Yet that is precisely the self-stultifying precept they are supposed to follow!

Legislation is such a complicated process today that, without experts familiar with what is going on in the myriad corridors of government, the individual citizen may not even know that his or her interests are at stake until it is too late to act. What pass for news media in most parts of the country are not informative about a legislative development until it has crystallized beyond the point where it can be readily modified. In order to bring informed citizen opinion to bear upon legislation while it is still malleable, alert and expert attention is required. Without an effective voluntary organization to arouse, mobilize, focus, and channel their concerns, citizens remain relatively impotent to effectuate them. The organization helps them to obtain information about their common concerns, to devise and implement a strategy to advance them, to amplify their views and coordinate their efforts, so that even a small number of citizens, when organized, can have an impact on events greater than a far larger number unorganized.

The First Amendment guarantees the right to *assemble* and to *petition the government for redress of grievances.* It is significant that the two activities are linked together in this one right—to assemble *and* to petition[5]—not that each may not occur independently of the other, but they reach their fullest effectiveness together: when citizens join to act in concert to affect the processes of government. There is nothing in the First Amendment—or anywhere else in the Constitution—that says each citizen must act alone and independently; quite the contrary. Yet the voluntary organizations (including churches) through which citizens seek to act in concert to advance the public interest are threatened with the loss of deductibility of contributions if they engage to any substantial degree in attempting to influence legislation! The only way they can retain deductibility is by eschewing the exercise of rights guaranteed by the Constitution.

Since most such organizations rely heavily upon the voluntary contributions of the citizens whose interests they seek to serve, the threat of the loss of deductibility can have a severely "chilling effect" upon the aggregate freedoms of speech, press, assembly, and petition of those citizens. For this reason, many people believe that the restriction on legislative activity by public charities (nonprofit voluntary organizations described in Section 501(c)(3)) is unconstitutional and

5. Cf. *U.S.* v. *Cruikshank,* 92 U.S. 542 (1876). Later cases have also recognized a "right of association" as a separate and independent right.

should be repealed. (The National Council of Churches in 1972, in testimony to the House Ways and Means Committee, urged this course.)

At long last, in 1976 Congress responded to the petitions of a coalition of public charities and in the so-called Tax Reform Act of that year redressed their grievances—in a way and to a degree. Congress did not do anything so forthright and foolhardy as deleting the objectionable limitation on influencing legislation, which still seems too attractive to many members of Congress to be cleanly eliminated. Instead, as is invariably the way in "tax reform," Congress piled one patch upon another, opening a very limited aperture through which certain organizations could do a controlled amount of restricted kinds of lobbying.

As is also characteristic of "tax reform," the particulars of the ostensible "reform" are so intricate and convoluted that it takes a tax lawyer to understand and utilize them—which is not so surprising in view of the fact that the revision in question was drafted by an armada of tax lawyers, some employed by the coalition of public charities, some by Congress, and some by the Treasury Department. But the main lines of this new wrinkle in the law are instructive for our purposes.

Over a number of years, the public charities' lobbying bill took various forms and was introduced in both houses by a succession of sponsors, the latest being Rep. Barber Conable (R-N.Y.). For several years it made little progress, partly because of the opposition of many churches—particularly the U.S. Catholic Conference. After repeated frustrations, the coalition of public charities finally perceived that it might be helpful to find out what was troubling the churches, and in a series of meetings certain revisions were agreed upon that met the concerns of the churches sufficiently for them to withdraw their opposition. Subsequently, the "Conable bill" was incorporated in the Tax Reform Act of 1976 and became law approximately in the form agreed upon.

The law adds a new Section 501(h), which permits certain public charities to *elect* to be covered by the new provision. For them, the term "substantial" in Section 501(c)(3) is—in effect—defined as an *expenditure* test, permitting them to expend up to a certain proportion of their total exempt-purpose expenditures for lobbying. The proportion is determined on a sliding scale, with organizations spending up to $500,000 on exempt purposes permitted to devote 20% of that amount to lobbying, and organizations spending over $1,500,000 permitted to spend $225,000 plus 5% of any amount over $1,500,000 for lobbying, up to a maximum of $1,000,000 in any taxable year. (The sliding scale is designed to reduce the advantage which large organizations would have over small ones if the same flat percentage applied to all.)

Within the permitted amount for lobbying, one-quarter (25%) can be used for "grass-roots" lobbying—attempting to influence legislation by attempting "to affect the opinion of the general public or any segment thereof." If an organization exceeds the permitted amounts, it is subject to a tax of 25% of the excess, and if it exceeds the limits by 50%, it forfeits its tax exemption under Section 501(c)(3). If it forfeits its exemption for this reason, it cannot slip over into Section 501(c)(4) and continue its exemption as an "action organization" (though no longer eligible for deductible contributions). (This rather stern provision is to prevent an organization from building up assets as a public charity and then using them for lobbying as an "action organization.")

Fortunately, an organization does not have to count as lobbying expenditures the costs of:

1. making available the results of nonpartisan analysis, study or research;
2. providing technical advice or assistance to a governmental body in response to a written request by it;
3. communications with legislative bodies on matters which might affect the organization's existence, powers, duties, or tax status;
4. communications between the organization and its bona fide members with respect to legislation of direct interest to it and them (so long as it does not urge or encourage the members to take specific actions to influence legislation or to enlist other persons to do so);
5. communications with government officials or employees not pertaining to legislation.

How would this work in practice? Let us suppose that the Audubon Society (which was instrumental in shaping this legislation) has an annual budget of $6,000,000, of which $500,000 is spent on fund-raising and $500,000 for capital expenditures—neither of which counts toward the basic amount ("exempt purpose expenditures")—so that basic amount is $5,000,000. The Audubon Society could then spend $400,000 on lobbying, of which one-quarter (25%) or $100,000 could be spent on grass-roots lobbying (trying to influence the general public). If the organization's budget for exempt purposes increased to $25,000,000, it could spend $1,000,000 on lobbying; if its budget increased to $100,000,000, it could still spend only $1,000,000 on lobbying in any taxable year.

Of that amount, from $750,000 to $1,000,000 could be spent on testimony before Congressional committees considering legislation on wildlife conservation, for instance, or on letters from the organization to committee members or employees, or on meetings with them to negotiate amendments. But only $250,000 could be spent on maga-zine, newspaper, or television advertisements urging readers or view-ers to support or oppose the legislation. If the organization wrote to its regular, dues-paying ("bona fide") members about the legislation, giving an objective pro-and-con treatment without advice on what to do about it, presumably the cost of the mailing would not count against the total available for lobbying; if the letter suggested that members write their Senators to oppose a particular amendment, it would count.

Some organizations are not enthusiastic about the new law, either because they do not contemplate doing much lobbying or because they are unhappy with the law's limitations—such as that on grass-roots lobbying. If so, they need not elect to be covered by the new law, but may remain under the old. Most churches which took an interest in the subject felt they were better off under existing law—ambiguous as it is. Believing that the limitation on lobbying is unconstitutional to begin with, they did not feel that grudging efforts to make it a little more palatable were genuine improvements, and might in fact be detriments in the long run. Therefore, they easily persuaded the spon-sors of the "Conable bill" to exclude churches from it altogether. But that was not enough, since there were still at least two reasons why churches felt they would be disadvantaged by it, even though ostensi-bly excluded: (1) because of the "bleed-through" of definitions of "substantial," and (2) because of "re-enactment" of the *Christian Echoes* decision.

(1) Even though an organization might not elect to be covered by the new law on lobbying, or even though churches might be excluded from it, they still might be affected by its definition of "substantial" because there is no other. The new law indicates that the test of "substantiality" is an *expenditure* test, and that it is a *proportionate* one. Furthermore, it predicates that in such a test *grass-roots lobbying counts four times as heavily as "direct" lobbying* (that which is carried on *directly* between the organization and legislators on subjects of *direct* interest to the organization).

Since churches are concerned to express their views on moral issues to *everyone,* not just to their members or to legislators, and since everything that affects the well-being of human beings is of direct interest to churches, they did not want to have those strictures projected upon them. So there is a clause in the new law stipulating that nothing in it will be construed to affect the interpretation of the phrase "no substantial part of the activities of which is . . . attempting to influence legislation" for organizations not electing, or not eligible, to be covered by it.

(2) There is a rule in interpreting legislation that if it is amended or extended by Congress following a judicial interpretation of a given section or clause, and Congress does not reject, correct, or modify that interpretation, it is, in effect, "re-enacted" into the law. That would have been the case with Section 501(c)(3)'s strictures on influencing legislation, which were construed by the Tenth Circuit Court of Appeals in the 1972 decision in *Christian Echoes National Ministry, Inc.,* v. *United States* (470 F.2d 849)—the only recent case dealing with a "church" whose tax exemption was revoked for "lobbying." That case and its outcome are of great importance to the topic of this chapter.

Billy James Hargis is a vehemently anti-Communist fundamentalist radio preacher whose headquarters are in Oklahoma. In the early 1960s the Internal Revenue Service directed its attentions to his continuous fulminations against the legislative programs of the Kennedy administration, the Service acting apparently at the behest of that administration. Local and then regional auditors found no reason for revoking his exemption, but Washington sent for the file and found the opposite to be the case, and his exemption was revoked. Hargis paid Social Security taxes under protest for several years and then sued for refund. The District Court found in his favor in 1971, determining, first, that Hargis's corporation, Christian Echoes National Ministry, was indeed a "church" for purposes of the tax law (though the Internal Revenue Service had taken it on precisely because it was *not* a church; Hargis has a church building and a local congregation which operate under another of his corporations), and second, that neither the government nor the courts had any business scrutinizing the operation and "work product" of a church to determine what part of it was "political" and what part "religious" for the purpose of concluding that the political part was "substantial" and therefore incompatible with the tax law.

On appeal, the government conceded that Hargis was indeed "religious" but that Section 501(c)(3) forbids substantial lobbying activity whatever its "motivation." The Tenth Circuit Court reversed the District Court and upheld the position of the government. Hargis appealed to the U.S. Supreme Court; and the National Council of Churches—which had long been one of Hargis's favorite targets—supported his position in a friend-of-the-court brief, pointing to the many respects in which the Tenth Circuit had disregarded the Supreme Court's carefully written opinion in the *Walz* case, and defending Hargis's right to preach what he felt called to preach (including denunciation of the National Council of Churches) without losing his tax exemption. Unfortunately, the Supreme Court declined to hear the case (which does not mean that it approves—or disapproves—the lower court's decision, which is left standing).

The thrust of the Tenth Circuit's opinion is conveyed in these words about the relationship between lobbying and tax exemption:

> In light of the fact that tax exemption is a privilege, a matter of grace rather than right, we hold that the limitations contained in Section 501(c)(3) withholding exemption from nonprofit corporations [which engaged in lobbying] do not deprive Christian Echoes of its constitutionally guaranteed right of free speech. The taxpayer may engage in all such activities without restraint, subject, however, to withholding of the exemp-

tion, or, in the alternative, the taxpayer may refrain from such activities and obtain the privilege of exemption.[6]

Thus, organizations—and particularly churches—are told by the court that they must choose between lobbying and tax exemption![7] In its brief *amicus curae* urging the Supreme Court to review that decision, the National Council of Churches pointed out three respects in which the Tenth Circuit contradicted the Supreme Court's opinion in the *Walz* case, which the Tenth Circuit apparently had not read, since it nowhere refers to it. (1) The Tenth Circuit refers to tax exemption as a "subsidy," which is a concept explicitly rejected by the Supreme Court in *Walz;* (2) it considers tax exemption to be provided to religious bodies in recognition of the social services they provide, which the Supreme Court also explicitly rejected in *Walz;* and (3) it treats "the participation by religious organizations in public affairs not as a full right under the First Amendment, but instead as a threat to the wall separating church and state. . . ." The Supreme Court, however, had said in *Walz* that such activity of churches is not only proper but is their *right:*

> Adherents of particular faiths and individual churches frequently take strong positions on public issues including, as this case reveals in the several briefs amici, vigorous advocacy of legal or constitutional positions. Of course, churches as much as secular bodies and private citizens have that right. 397 U.S. at 670.[8]

More important, the National Council of Churches' friend-of-the-court brief maintains that tax exemption is not a "privilege" but an essential safeguard of the free exercise of religion. But whether tax exemption is a right or a privilege, insists the National Council of Churches' brief, it cannot be conditioned upon surrendering a right guaranteed by the Constitution (citing *Sherbert* v. *Verner* 374 U.S.

6. *Christian Echoes National Ministry, Inc.,* v. *U.S.,* 470 F.2d at 857 (1972).

7. As pointed out earlier, the choice posed is actually between lobbying and deductibility of contributions.

8. Quotations are from the National Council of Churches' *amicus* brief. See also Clark, Elias, "The Limitation on Political Activities: A Discordant Note in the Law of Charities" 46 *Virginia Law Review* 439–466 (1960) and Burns, W. Peter, "Constitutional Aspects of Church Taxation" in 9 *Columbia Journal of Law and Social Problems* 646–680 (1973).

398 (1963) and *Speiser* v. *Randall* 357 U.S. 513 (1958)), nor can it operate to prefer churches which speak out on public issues over those which do not (citing the ban on laws which "prefer one religion over another" in *Everson* v. *Board of Education* 330 U.S. 1, 16 (1947)). The chief vice of the Tenth Circuit's opinion is that it sets a condition on the churches' tax exemption: *they must keep silent on public issues in order to qualify!* It is a tragedy that the Supreme Court did not correct this grotesque decision, which hangs like a sword of Damocles over the heads of all the churches and which the Internal Revenue Service can invoke at any time against any of them that engage in "substantial" lobbying.

Such, then, was the judicial (mis)interpretation of Section 501(c)(3) which the churches did not want "re-enacted" by Congress. They were successful in getting a specific disclaimer written into the statute itself (over the vehement objections of the Treasury):

> It is the intent of Congress that enactment of this section is not to be regarded in any way as an approval or disapproval of the decision of the Court of Appeals for the Tenth Circuit in Christian Echoes National Ministry, Inc. versus United States, 470 F.2d 849 (1972), or of the reasoning in any of the opinions leading to that decision.

This disclaimer means that the *Christian Echoes* decision is binding only in the Tenth Circuit and is not "the law of the land," as it might otherwise have been.[9]

One reason churches were wary of being included in the public charities' legislation was that it afforded additional scope to bureau-

9. For federal court purposes, the United States is divided into eleven "circuits." The decisions of one circuit do not bind the other circuits, unless ratified by the United States Supreme Court.

Although the Tenth Circuit's decision in *Christian Echoes* may not command much respect by itself, there has been one troublesome Supreme Court development in the parochial school-aid cases that may lend some additional credence to the constitutionality of restrictions on political activity by churches. See the discussion of "political divisiveness along religious lines" in *Lemon* v. *Kurtzman,* 403 U.S. 602 (1971), *Committee for Public Education and Religious Liberty* v. *Nyquist,* 413 U.S. 756 (1973), and *Meek* v. *Pittenger,* 421 U.S. 349 (1975). Although it is not exactly clear what the Supreme Court means by the "political divisiveness" passages in these decisions, churches should be alert to prevent any "bleed-through" from these passages concerning Roman Catholic advocacy of aid to parochial schools to broader advocacy by the Roman Catholic or other churches on matters of more general interest in other public affairs.

cratic investigation, regulation, and restriction of citizen activity. They saw how—bit by bit—the 1934 limitation on lobbying and the 1954 limitation on electioneering had been interpreted by the Internal Revenue Service to be a ban on "political" activity of any kind, a license to beat back all forms of organizing or agitating that had a disquieting effect on the public scene and which benefited in any way from tax exemption.

"When "public-interest law firms" began to litigate issues of civil rights, consumer welfare, and environmental protection, the Internal Revenue Service cracked down on them for engaging in "political activity," though there is nothing in the exemption sections that refers to litigation at all. Litigation is not "attempting to influence legislation" nor is it "interfering in . . . campaigns for public office." But it was not until a concerted campaign by several Senators resulted in public hearings that the then Commissioner of Internal Revenue, Randolph Thrower, was willing to admit "public-interest law firms" to the privileged precincts of the "law of charities."

Other examples of the restrictive use of the tax law to keep public charities and even churches out of the public-policy ("political") arena were cited in a report to the governing board of the National Council of Churches in the early 1970s:[10]

1. IRS advised the Episcopal Church that the use of a designated offering for a student political education program would jeopardize the denomination's tax exemption.

2. IRS investigated the use of space in Trinity Episcopal Church in Melrose, Massachusetts, by a student peace group and warned the church that such use was not compatible with its tax exemption.

3. IRS has made inquiries of the Florida and California Migrant Ministries about their tax exemption following their vigorous support of the efforts of Cesar Chavez and the United Farm Workers to organize agricultural workers (there was no legislation on the subject of agricultural labor being advocated by them at that time, nor was Chavez running for public office, but there was a highly publicized boycott of table grapes, which may have seemed to IRS to smack of "political" activity).

4. IRS sent written reminders that political activity is contrary to

10. Dean M. Kelley, "New Developments in Relations Between Church and State."

Section 501(c)(3) of the Internal Revenue Code to the National Council of Churches and to the Office of Communications of the United Church of Christ shortly after these two organizations had requested an opportunity to testify before a Senate Committee chaired by Senator John O. Pastore (D-R.I.) against a bill sponsored by him that would insure automatic renewal of broadcast licenses to incumbent licensees; needless to say, the two groups testified anyway, and nothing further was heard from IRS.

5. A settlement house in California, owned and operated by a United Presbyterian mission agency, was investigated by IRS, which allowed the settlement house to keep its exemption despite certain "objectionable activities" if it would go, and sin no more. The list of activities deemed "objectionable" by IRS is revealing:

> We have completed our examination of your records for the years ended February 28, 1968, 1969, and 1970. No change in your exempt status is necessary.
>
> However, we noted that, in the past, you have conducted seven activities which are objectionable to the status of an organization exempt under section 501(c)(3) of the Internal Revenue Code of 1954. These activities are:
>
> 1. Your facilities were used to plan a demonstration.
> 2. Your vehicle was used to transport pickets to a demonstration.
> 3. Your vehicle was used to transport several of your employees to a convention in Denver, Colorado. There is no evidence in your records to show that the purpose of the trip constituted an exempt activity.
> 4. Your facilities were used by the Mexican American Political Association.
> 5. You were associated with the Congress of Mexican American Unity. The Mexican American Association has as one of its purposes the selection and endorsement of political candidates.
> 6. During the years under examination, you adopted a general program of "community involvement" without notifying the District Director of Internal Revenue of the change in your operations.
> 7. Records were not maintained to show that activities of your executive director and community organizers were in furtherance of your exempt purpose.

All of these activities are specifically prohibited by Section 501(c)(3) of the Code and the regulations thereunder.

Your exempt status may be adversely affected in future periods if you continue to perform any of the prohibited acts mentioned above.

Thank you for your cooperation.

Very truly yours,
(signed)
District Director

January 14, 1972

Far from being "prohibited," at least some of these activities would seem to be permissible under Treasury regulations defining "charitable" as used in Section 501(c)(3)—regulations adopted after an adverse ruling by a court corrected Treasury's interpretation by explaining that such activities as the following are indeed "charitable":

—Relief of the poor and distressed or of the underprivileged;
—Advancement of religion, advancement of education or science;
—Erection or maintenance of public buildings, monuments or works;
—Lessening of the burdens of government;
—Promotion of social welfare by organizations designed to accomplish any
    of the above purposes, or
    (i) to lessen neighborhood tensions;
    (ii) to eliminate prejudice and discrimination;
    (iii) to defend human and civil rights secured by law;
    (iv) to combat community deterioration and juvenile delinquency;

The fact that an organization, in carrying out its primary purposes, advocates social or civic changes or presents opinion on controversial issues with the intent of molding public opinion or creating public sentiment to an acceptance of its views does not [disqualify an organization for exemption].

Reg. Sec. 1.501(c)(3)—1(d)(2)

The churches, in considering whether to avail themselves of the limited opportunity for permissible direct lobbying offered by the public charities' legislation, could not imagine that the sort of scrutiny and supervision just described would be *less* if they subjected themselves to the bill's elaborate provisions for expenditure tests, communications limited to "bona fide members," and restrictions on "grass-roots lobbying." So they perferred the evil they knew to the one they didn't.

Another reason churches resisted inclusion in the new law was that they have never conceded that what *they* do with respect to public policy *is* "lobbying" in the usual or historic sense of that term. "Lobbying" is a term originally applied to well-heeled agents of business or other private interests who waited in the "lobby" of the legislature to buttonhole legislators and persuade them to vote in such a way that the private self-interests represented by the "lobbyists" would be advanced or at least not impaired. In most instances, what churches urge upon the public as a whole—including legislators—is not necessarily in the churches' own self-interest as organizations but rather is directed to the common good—whether or not they benefit from it as organizations. Churches are bound by their sense of mission, their consecrated obedience to God, to speak out on issues where the well-being of human persons is at stake, to proclaim what they believe is the right and moral course for the whole society and what will benefit everyone, not just themselves or their members. Churches were doing this sort of thing long before there were legislatures or lobbies, and they will continue to do so—despite whatever odds or obstacles—as long as there are churches.

For this reason, most churches, as such, have not registered under existing laws designed to identify and regulate "lobbyists," nor have their agencies—at least those that are integrally related to churches—since the very act of registration of lobbyists would seem to put them in jeopardy under the lobbying limitation of Section 501(c)(3).

Some churches have contemplated setting up non-exempt affiliates to carry on lobbying activities; the Friends Committee on National Legislation has never sought 501(c)(3) status and has always been a registered "lobbyists" related to but not controlled by the Religious Society of Friends (Quakers). This tactic of creating "hard-money" subsidiaries for lobbying purposes may become necessary for churches someday, but most of them will continue to resist this bifurcation of their mission into what is exempt and what is non-exempt because of the implication that the former is somehow more hallowed than the latter and because of the danger of divergence between the two that has befallen several other parallel arrangements, such as the NAACP and the NAACP Legal Defense Fund, which have become two separate and independent organizations, one "deductible" and the other not.

Throughout the history of the nation—and long before—churches have been active in helping to shape the public policy of the commonwealth in ways they believed God desired. They were instrumental in setting the stage for the obtaining of independence at its beginning, when "the black regiment"—as James Otis called them—of the dissenting clergy thundered against the tyranny of King George from their pulpits.[11] A few decades later, the churches, acting corporately, brought an end to the practices of dueling by getting prohibitions against it written into the constitutions of twenty-one states,[12] and no one conceived that this activity had any bearing on their tax exemption. Churches were active in the effort to abolish slavery (though by the time of the Civil War there were religious apologists *for* slavery in the churches of the South). Churches pressed for laws against gambling, Sabbath-breaking, alcoholic beverages, prostitution, and child labor. They have worked for laws advancing labor organizing, woman suffrage, civil rights, and family welfare.

In none of these instances—prior to the amendment of the tax law in 1934—was such public-spirited activity of the churches conceived to jeopardize their tax exemption. Nor should it today. Quite the contrary: it is to the benefit of the civil discourse in a democracy that moral issues and considerations should be put forward in the most forthright fashion by dedicated organizations having a long history, worldwide perspective, and relatively little self-interest in the outcome. The churches serve the public good by their participation in the civil discourse, and instead of being penalized for it by loss of tax exemption, they should be encouraged. In fact, we might almost contend that if churches were to lose tax exemption for anything, it should be for *failing* to attempt to "influence legislation"!

But this would be to impose a "sectarian" and essentially extraneous expectation on religious bodies. Though most Christian groups

11. See Dean M. Kelley, "Religion in the American Revolution," *Christianity and Crisis,* Vol. 34, No. 10, June 10, 1974.

12. Anson Phelps Stokes, *Church and State in the United States,* (New York: Harper & Bros., 1950), Vol. II, Chapters 14–16.

consider it part of their religious duty to evince a concern for the condition of the commonwealth and to act upon that concern in ways they believe will better the commonwealth, that is not a universal or essential element in the religious enterprise. Many religious bodies fulfill the religious function quite effectively without busying themselves in public affairs, and that is the conclusive consideration. Tax exemption helps to shield and foster the important function of religion, and whether legislation is influenced or not should have nothing to do with it.

7

Tax Exemption Need Not Be Unlimited

Sometimes the question is asked, "Aren't the churches concerned about the shrinking tax base?" The answer is that, of course, they are. One evidence of such concern would be the misconceived *mea culpa* of Dr. Shriver cited in the first chapter. Another would be the policy statements adopted by several denominations and councils of churches (two are quoted in Chapter 1) which suggest limitations or alternatives to the present arrangement, such as voluntary payments in lieu of taxes by churches or assessment of service charges by municipalities. Probably the most notable indication of concern is the joint action by the National Council of Churches and the U.S. Catholic Conference to close the "loophole" for exemption of unrelated business income of churches, which Congress wrote into the Tax Reform Act of 1969. Let those criticize the churches who have themselves given up a tax preference from which they ostensibly benefit!

But the churches' concern about the "shrinking tax base" does not necessarily require them to rush to Caesar to be taxed. Such a course would be to fall in with popular misconceptions on this theme rather than correcting them. Foremost among them is the fallacy that the "tax base" is "shrinking," a characterization that is accurate only if one looks in isolation at certain taxing jurisdictions and methods, such as the property tax in a deteriorating center-city whose wealthier citizens have moved to the suburbs. But there are other methods of taxation and broader jurisdictions.

The United States is a rich nation, whose gross national product is increasing year by year. If the wealth which it creates cannot be more adequately and justly and directly applied to the public needs of the nation, the fault is not the churches, and they should not be made the scapegoats for the nation's apparent willingness to tolerate increasing public penury in the midst of private affluence. Exempt entities (the largest categories of which are *not* churches) are simply not the place to look for significant public revenues to meet the costs of the commonwealth. Only an adequate and straightforward system of income taxation of the sources or producers of wealth will do that, and all other methods are "gimmicks" which tend to divert attention from that basic truth.

Unfortunately, many legislators and leaders of American public life are unwilling to "bite the bullet" of taxing the main reservoirs of wealth in proportion to their ability to pay and instead resort to gimmicks, some of which—like sales taxes—are regressive and others —like lotteries—are socially destructive. And one of the most spurious and potentially damaging gimmicks is the pointing of greedy fingers at exempt entities with the implication that in them is a vast untapped and "privileged" source of revenue. It is spurious because they are not producers of wealth but consumers. It is potentially damaging to the entire social fabric of the commonwealth because— if they were (mistakenly) to be taxed—their ability to stimulate and undergird and embody the network of voluntary public-spirited activity of citizens would be impaired, if not destroyed. And with what gain?

Many of the services performed and activities undertaken by exempt organizations are at least as meritorious and constructive as those for which tax funds are appropriated by the legislatures of the land. Just because government has the power to tax does not mean that governmental expenditures are of greater value, wisdom, effectiveness, or importance than nongovernmental ones; often quite the opposite. And citizens who try to carry out such constructive nongovernmental voluntary undertakings should be encouraged rather than penalized for doing so. They each already pay their (presumably) fair share of taxes; they should not be taxed again for what they voluntarily contribute to endeavors that help to strengthen the fabric of society (and which, in the case of churches, may also be performing an essential social function). Instead, they should be encouraged in such activities by the neutral, self-assessing, and self-allocating incentives of tax exemption and deductibility of contributions.

Views similar to those expressed here were enunciated in 1969 by Boris I. Bittker, Sterling Professor of Law at the Yale Law School, an outstanding authority on tax policy. In a classic law-review article, "Churches, Taxes and the Constitution," he refutes the critics of tax exemption of churches on two points:

> In my view, the anti-exemption case is much weaker than has been recognized. Defenders of the status quo have failed to put their best foot forward because they have conceded too readily the validity of two essential but unarticulated premises on which the anti-exemption case rests:
>
> 1. That the term "tax exemption" has so self-evident a meaning that it need not be subjected to analysis; and
>
> 2. That tax exemptions *ipso facto* relieve religious organizations or their members from paying their "fair share" of government expenditures. . . .
>
> A close examination of the nature of tax exemption reveals a serious weakness in the contention that exemptions automatically serve to establish religion. There is no way to tax *everything;* a legislative body, no matter how avid for revenue, can do no more than pick out from the universe of people, entities, and events over which it has jurisdiction those that, in its view, are appropriate objects of taxation. In specifying the ambit of any tax, the legislature cannot avoid "exempting" those persons, events, activities or entities that are outside the territory of the proposed tax. In describing a tax's boundaries, the draftsman may choose to make the exclusions explicit ("All property except that owned by nonprofit organizations"), or implicit ("all property owned by organizations operated for profit"), but either way, the result is the same—taxpayers are separated from nontaxpayers. . . .
>
> The federal income tax of current law, then, "exempts" nonprofit groups; and this quite naturally leads, on a quick glance, to the conclusion that they have been granted the "privilege" of "immunity." . . . Unless blinded by labels, however, one can view the federal income tax instead as

a tax on income that inures in measurable amounts to the direct or indirect personal benefit of identifiable natural persons. So viewed, the Internal Revenue Code's "exemption" of nonprofit organizations is simply a way of recognizing the inapplicability to them of a concept that is central to the tax itself.[1]

(An analysis in the same article of the concept of "fair share" as applied to churches likewise reduces it to absurdity.)

The argument has been made in earlier chapters that churches have additional justification for not being taxed. Not only are they non-wealth-producing voluntary entities which also perform a function necessary to the survival of society as a whole, but they render as a by-product of their basic function (the provision of ultimate meaning) a continuing value assessment or legitimation of the governing authorities. This by-product, legitimation, is not well understood even by the sociologists and political scientists who discerned it. It is not something that religious groups can turn on or off at will, or direct consciously for or against a given target. But over an extended period of time, and largely unconsciously, people derive from their basic framework of ultimate meaning a sense that it is right (or not right) to obey, affirm, and be loyal to a certain system of authority (or legitimated power). Without this sense of ought-ness or legitimacy in the minds of most of the people, a ruler cannot rule; there are not enough policemen to keep an eye on everyone if the people are not to a large extent self-policing—which means accepting of legitimated authority.

A historic shift in legitimation took place at the birth of this nation. Over the course of a century and a half the inhabitants of these shores changed their way of thinking about the authority of the British king. In the Mayflower Compact of 1620, the Pilgrims characterized themselves as "loyal servants of our dread sovereign Lord, King James." Yet in 1776 the Declaration of Independence could say of his successor, George III, "A prince whose character is thus marked by every act which may define a tyrant is unfit to be the ruler of a free people." It was not just the colonists' experience with British rule that caused the change but the *interpretation* of that experience in its spiritual

1. 78 *Yale Law Journal* at 1287, 1288, 1290, 1291 (1969).

significance thundered from a thousand pulpits, comparing the King to a wicked Pharaoh trying to hinder the Children of Israel in their "errand into the wilderness," their occupation of the Promised Land.

The clergy were not alone in this work, of course; politicians and pamphleteers, journalists and philosophers were likewise denouncing King and Parliament. But the transition from "loyal servants" to "a free people" and from "dread sovereign Lord" to a prince unfit to rule was part of the colonists' self-understanding, rooted in and derived from their understanding of broader and deeper matters: the nature and destiny of humankind, the purpose and will of God, the ultimate meaning of life. Thus it was a religious or quasi-religious outcome, regardless of who brought it about. And it is not surprising that the persons and organizations to which the people looked for their understanding of ultimate meaning should also help them to form their assessment of earthly authority and their allegiance to it. As Sydney Ahlstrom noted, the "colonial clergy addressing large, regular audiences from positions of great prestige was a major force in arousing the spirit of independence after 1761,"[2] and the thrust of the process of legitimation (or delegitimation) is best summed up by one who lived through it, John Adams:

> What do we mean by the American Revolution? Do we mean the American war? The Revolution was effected before the war commenced. The Revolution was in the minds and hearts of the people, *a change in their religious sentiments of their duties and obligations.* . . .[3]

As was pointed out in Chapter 4, rulers through the ages have tried to insure themselves legitimation by winning the favor of existing religions or instituting new ones, but these captive or symbiotic relationships have not always been persuasive to those beginning to doubt because the religious voice did not seem to be giving independent testimony. Legitimation is more convincing when it comes (as a by-product) from an independent and disinterested witness. Churches are able to offer a more effective value assessment of the ruling authority if they are not dependent upon it or subordinate to it. For this reason,

2. *A Religious History of the American People* (New Haven, Conn.: Yale University Press, 1972), p. 361.
3. John Adams, Letter to Hezekiah Niles, 1818, emphasis added.

a condition almost of "extraterritoriality" has developed in this nation, in which churches have a special status with respect to government—ineligible for support by government and (to a remarkable degree) immune from pressures to support it by legitimation or taxes.

This "extraterritoriality" is neither absolute nor infinite. No more than the United Nations headquarters or the embassies of foreign powers is the property and operation of a church totally isolated from the surrounding community. And the amount of territory available to a given religious body need not be entirely open-ended. There may be appropriate limitations or exceptions to non-taxability, for instance, to which we should give some consideration.

The National Council of Churches, in its policy statement TAX EXEMPTION OF CHURCHES, recognizes the possibility of limitation:

> In the United States, it has been a basic public policy since the founding of the nation to accord to freedom of religion, speech, press and assembly a "preferred position" at the head of the Bill of Rights. Christians support and affirm this healthful arrangement of the civil order, not solely or primarily for themselves and their churches, but for everyone. Citizens, whatever their beliefs, should likewise appreciate the policy of our society that the free exercise of religion cannot be licensed or taxed by government.[4] Property or income of religious bodies that is genuinely necessary (rather than merely advantageous) to the free exercise of religion should likewise not be taxed. Except for cases where exemption is required to afford equality with other eleemosynary institutions, such exemption should be confined to the essential facilities of the church and to the voluntary contributions of the faithful for the operation of the religious organization.[5]

There are conceivably various expenditures by churches that are *not* essential to the free exercise of religion, such as speculative investments, which might be subject to taxation just as income from trade or business unrelated to the exempt function of a church now is. Of

4. The statement is referring to decisions by the U.S. Supreme Court such as *Murdock* v. *Pennsylvania,* 319 US 105 (1943), and *Follett* v. *McCormick,* 321 US 573 (1944).

5. Adopted by the General Board of the NCC May 2, 1969. See Appendix B for full text.

course, a church should always be permitted to attempt to show that a given type of expenditure proposed to be taxed is indeed essential to the free exercise of religion of its members.

What kinds of limitations might apply? Reference has already been made to limitations of *purpose,* which are already in effect in many jurisdictions. That is, property is not exempt from taxation unless it is used for exempt *purposes.* Most jurisdictions test both *ownership* and actual *use* of property to determine this point. It is not enough that property is owned by a church; it must also be *used* for exempt purposes. If it is used for *commercial* purposes, it is taxed in most jurisdictions, even though the *income* from such use may go to support the church. (That income, too, is now taxable, if it is "active,"[6] under the Internal Revenue Code amendments of 1969 urged by the National Council of Churches and the U.S. Catholic Conference.)

Land that is owned by a church but not used at all (undeveloped) is also taxed in most jurisdictions, though some allow a period of grace during which the church may build upon it without incurring tax, such as five or ten years. In some jurisdictions, parsonages are taxed, in others, not. In some, parking lots contiguous to the church are taxed, in others, not. A running battle is going on in Nashville, Tennessee, and other places over whether church-owned publishing firms are taxable on the non-religious portion of their property or product. Church-owned campgrounds are also a bone of contention, particularly if they include a large area of undeveloped land and are used only during a few months of the year.

Churches could probably survive taxation of parsonages, publishing houses, and parking lots (though when a municipality will not issue a building permit unless the plan includes a specified number of off-street parking spaces per 100 members, the parking lot has been determined by the municipality itself to be indispensable) and should be able to distinguish between them and more central uses. If a legal battle must be joined on whether church property can be taxed, let

6. Churches, like other Section 501(c)(3) organizations, do not have to pay federal income taxes on "passive" income (such as dividends and interest from investments). But if they "actively" engage in the regular conduct of a commercial trade or business, they must pay the federal tax on "unrelated business income." For special rules on "debt-financed income," including investment income, see Section 514 of the Internal Revenue Code.

it be on some more central issue, such as that posed in *Walz* v. *Tax Commission,* where the exemption of the house of worship itself was at stake, or in *Christian Echoes National Ministry, Inc.* v. *U.S.,* where the right of a religious group to engage in lobbying without losing its tax exemption was called into question.

There is another kind of limitation or mitigation of tax exemption which is in use in various jurisdictions, and that is some mode of compensation by churches for municipal services they enjoy. The rationale set forth earlier, that citizens who already pay their fair share of taxes should not be taxed again for voluntary collective activities from which they derive no profit, has an important corollary: that those collective activities should not themselves impose an additional burden on the taxpayers. That is, those who wish to join together to operate a club, a private school, a museum, or a library should defray any costs which the existence and operation of that facility actually causes the municipality, and there is no reason churches should not be covered by the same principle. They should pay the actual cost of any municipal services they need and use (and which would not otherwise be necessary).

This principle is different from the concept of "voluntary payments in lieu of taxes" advocated by some church people, presumably following the model of payments made by some governmental agencies (state and federal) to municipalities where agency facilities are located. But the church is not another government with its own taxing powers, and the model is defective in this respect, as well as posing hazards for churches which are listed in Chapter 1. But a service charge is not a tax and would be perfectly appropriate if it represents the exact expense caused or incurred by the church, such as a paving assessment per frontage-foot, water-rent per gallon metered to the church, or charges for electricity per kilowatt-hour actually used. (Deriving a measured charge for sewerage might be more difficult.) There is no reason why churches should not "pay their own way" in this realistic sense. They do not need or ask special favors like free water or electricity for which others have to pay.

But genuine service charges are entirely different from paying a proportion of the whole municipal budget, which is not significantly increased by the presence of churches, and indeed might be greater if they were *not* there. The difference can be seen in the distinction between paying a crossing guard by the hour to assist and protect persons entering and leaving the church at hours of service, on the one hand, and paying some proportion of the total cost of the whole police force, on the other. The police department as a whole would operate with much the same scope, methods, and expenses if the church were replaced by a pizza parlor or haberdashery; the church's existence and location is not a significant factor in determining the police department's budget and so it should not be chargeable to the church. The same can be said of the fire department, the sanitation department, the health department, the welfare department, the school board, etc. Service charges should be connected dollar-for-dollar with expenses actually attributable to the church, and the church should have no reluctance on principle to paying them.

Another type of limitation might be a *quantitative* one. A municipal government might conceivably set limits on the amount or value of property that would be untaxed to a congregation of a certain size. What would be a reasonable limitation? Suppose a church with a thousand members wishes to build a new church on a three-acre plot. Is that an excessive area? If a public high school in the same municipality is required to secure a site of not less than three acres for a thousand students, the church's plans—in the absence of a showing by the municipality that the needs of a church and a high school are not commensurate—would seem to be not unreasonable.

There are various difficulties with this mode of limitation. If it is based on the size of the congregation, does the tax assessor approach as the congregation dwindles? Does he retreat if it expands? But a building site and the edifice upon it do not shrink or swell as elastically as the membership, so a building constructed to fit within the exemption limitation at the time of construction probably should not be subject to a lesser limit later, even if the number in the congregation using it should decrease over the years.

A limitation based on value is less justifiable. What is mainly objected to is the accumulation of land by exempt entities, thus removing it from the total floor space of the municipality available for profit-making, taxable uses. Whether a church builds an expensive structure or a more modest one is of less importance than the acreage it takes out of taxation. Furthermore, if the value of the property happens to increase over the years because of factors over which the church has no control, it might face taxation at some point through no fault of its own.

In any event, with this type of limitation—area or value or both— the church should be taxed at prevailing rates only on the amount of property by which it exceeds the limit. It would always have a basic beachhead of exempt property within which to operate.

It is conceivable that exempt property in a given jurisdiction might come to exceed taxable property.[7] Tax assessors are often heard to lament that such is virtually the case already—by which they often mean that exempt property is approaching 10% or 20% of the total area!—but if exempt property were actually to exceed 50%, then drastic steps might indeed become necessary. Of course, the first and most obvious of these is usually overlooked: the jurisdiction is too narrow and should be expanded, perhaps by amalgamation with neighboring jurisdictions. But since that would mean the loss of many

7. Such was the condition alleged to prevail in Hardenburgh Township, Ulster County, New York. *The New York Times* saw fit to run this story under a two-column head and picture on the front page of its Sunday edition on September 19, 1976, proclaiming: "Half of Town's Residents Ordained to Qualify for Tax-Exempt Status." Some of the 236 residents, the story asserts, pay "as much as two-thirds of their meager incomes" in taxes because of the purchase of scenic properties by Zen Buddhists, Boy Scouts, Tibetan monks, and other exempt organizations. Eventually, the story reveals that the exempt property is only $5 million out of a total of $21 million assessed valuation. Half of the residents were reported to have been ordained by the "bishop" of the "Universal Life Church"—a 41-year-old plumber from Liberty, N.Y. *The New York Times* story does not disclose how this flood-tide of religious zeal would benefit the residents in regard to taxes except to draw the attention of the legislature to their plight. Ordained clergymen have to pay property taxes on property they own, so ordination would be of no advantage in that respect. New York state does afford ordained clergypersons a $1,500 reduction on their assessed valuation, a tax saving of $20 or $30 a year (depending upon the tax rate and the valuation of the property), but only if the ordained person is engaged in *full-time* religious ministry—which the good folk of Hardenburgh do not pretend to be.

A more recent account (*New York Times,* December 5, 1976) indicated that some of the newly-ordained "clergy" planned to organize their families into "congregations" and to hold periodic worship services in their homes, thus ostensibly converting them into "churches" that would be exempt from property tax. The township's tax assessor seemed inclined to acquiesce in this fiction, and the rest of the state can only marvel at this new "Great Awakening" and wonder how far it will sweep, converting whole countrysides into clusters of instant house-churches, with who knows what transforming effect upon the moral and spiritual condition of the nation!

courthouse jobs in each jurisdiction, it does not offer much appeal to incumbents, and covetous eyes are once more turned upon the exempt entities as though they were the villains.

One mode of remedy—more drastic than the preceding one—would be to limit by law the proportion of acreage within the jurisdiction that would be available for exempt use, perhaps to the 50% level about which such alarm is expressed. When that limit was reached, any new exempt entities would have to purchase land from other, already exempt, landholders rather than taking additional land off the tax rolls. This arrangement, however, would pit one class of exempt property owner against another, with governmental bodies having power of condemnation which they could use to dispossess private exempt entities from their share of the exempt precinct. This mode of limitation would also place an added burden on new exempt organizations seeking to come into being.

Few jurisdictions in the United States have sought to place ceilings upon the extent of exempt property—either by the individual parcel or in the aggregate—but the possibility is not remote. Indeed, it is reminiscent of the European model of anti-mortmain statutes, such as were enacted in England as early as the thirteenth century. ("Mortmain" means "dead hand" and refers to the ability of corporations—including particularly churches—to own land in perpetuity since, unlike natural persons, they do not die.) Such statutes were directed at the church, which because of bequests and accumulations soon came to own vast estates, often comprising more than half the domain. In some cases, this condition led to outright confiscation—as when Henry VIII confiscated the monasteries in the sixteenth century and Mexico nationalized the churches in the twentieth. At other times such statutes limited the amount of property the church could own to what was absolutely necessary. Anti-mortmain statutes have never been extensive in the United States and have been considerably relaxed elsewhere. Nevertheless, they suggest a direction in which the law might move if the exemption situation becomes intolerable—or if alarmists convince people that it is—which may in the end be much the same thing.

8

Charitable Solicitations and Designated Contributions

In most of the states of the United States there is an official—usually the attorney general or the secretary of state—who is responsible for preventing or punishing frauds and other abuses in fund appeals soliciting charitable contributions from the public. Recent disclosures of the not-entirely-charitable uses of such contributions by Father Flanagan's Boys Town and the Pallottine Fathers have stimulated such officials to find ways to make organizations soliciting funds more accountable to the public. The principal pattern of abuse they seek to correct is that in which a large proportion of the funds collected is used for the costs of the appeal, for the overhead expenses of the sponsoring organization—some of which seem to have very little direct connection with remedying the needs portrayed in the solicitation—and for investments. (The Pallottine Fathers had made heavy speculative investments in Florida real estate and in loans—among others—to Governor Marvin Mandel of Maryland. Income from these investments was ostensibly to be used to further the missionary purposes for which the funds were originally solicited.)

One remedy often suggested, and being tried in some jurisdictions, is "Truth-in-Giving" laws, which require organizations undertaking charitable solicitations to register with the appropriate state official and to file a statement showing the past and/or proposed distribution of funds given by the public. That statement is then available for inspection by the public. In fact, the statement may be required to accompany any appeal to the public, whether by direct mail, newspaper advertisement, or door-to-door solicitation. A federal statute of this type has been proposed and may become law in the near future.

The raising of funds by charitable solicitation is big business, and a trade association of those engaged in this specialized line of work has been formed, called the American Association of Fund-Raising Counsel. At a recent conference of the National Association of Attorneys General devoted entirely to the subject of regulating charitable solicitations,[1] several members of the fund-raising profession were heard to protest that they were being viewed by the state officials as the "enemy" because of the size of their fees, which, they insisted, were not disproportionate to the time, effort, skill—and risk—involved. Still, it is arguable that when the costs of raising a given sum are greater than the amount realized for actual charitable use, the giving public might have an interest in knowing that fact—not that it is necessarily improper or culpable, but one might find it edifying to know what portion of one's contribution goes to the solicitor and what portion to charity.

But fund-raising counsel seem to resist the requirement of public disclosure on the supposition—probably justified—that if a potential giver is reminded of the obvious fact that not every penny of his donated dollar goes to the charitable purpose, he or she might be less inclined to contribute. It costs money to raise money, and however reasonable the expenses of a fund drive may be, to remind donors of that fact is often to put a drag on the drive's productivity. Consequently, it is not always easy to find out how much of the proceeds of a charitable campaign goes into "payload" and how much into the costs of the "pipeline"; that is one of the better-kept secrets of the fund-raising trade—unless its disclosure is required by law. Is such disclosure a good thing?

As noted earlier, fund-raising is big business. Major contributors are asked to make "leadership" gifts that "set the pace" for a large fund drive, and substantial amounts of money flow in before the drive is over. Charitable organizations and professional fund-raisers owe it

1. Miami Beach, Florida, where the main lines of this book were first presented in a paper on charitable solicitations.

to their own long-range interests to avoid even the *appearance* of hanky-panky by publishing audited accounts of what was done with every penny contributed to them. Churches are no exception to this consideration, so long as disclosure is voluntary. When it is required by law, churches should be exempted (for reasons to be summarized below), though the exemption need not include church-related schools, colleges, hospitals, homes, or similar religious agencies if they conduct their own fund-raising campaigns independently of the church. The Filer Commission makes a similar recommendation:

> That all larger tax-exempt charitable organizations *except churches and church affiliates* be required to prepare and make readily available detailed annual reports on their finances, programs and priorities.
>
> Reporting requirements that now apply only to private foundations should be broadened so that all 501(c)(3) and 501(c)(4) organizations with annual budgets of more than $100,000 are required to file annual reports. This requirement would not apply to religious organizations, although some Commission members feel that it should apply to nonsacramental activities of religious organizations such as hospitals and schools.[2]

Why should churches as such be exempted? This question has been dealt with repeatedly in previous chapters, and the answer—whether or not it is convincing to all—should by this time at least be clear: *Churches are engaged in a unique sort of activity which is:*

(a) of survival value to society as a whole;

(b) not susceptible to external evaluation;

(c) often weakened, distorted, or perverted by governmental interference, whether intended to hinder or to "help";

(d) adequately answerable to adherents so long as dependent upon voluntary contributions for support.[3]

2. *Giving in America,* p. 164, emphasis added.
3. "Bingo" and other such fund-raising functions are already taxable, if regularly carried on, as an unrelated "trade or business," unless substantially all of the work is done by volunteers. *Smith-Dodd Businessman's Association, Inc.* v. *Commissioner of Internal Revenue,* 65 T.C. 620 (1975). This is an important safeguard against a church's relying increasingly upon commercial expedients rather than upon the voluntary support of its adherents (which can be in the form of volunteer labor as well as contributions of money).

Giving to churches is the largest single category of private philanthropy in this nation. In 1972, "religion" received twice or thrice as much in voluntary giving as any of the other major categories used by the Filer Commission (the "twice or thrice" depends on whether "nonsacramental uses" are included in the religious category or redistributed among other categories):

"WHERE THE GIVING GOES"†

Distribution of Private Philanthropy by Recipient, 1972
(In billions of dollars)

	Standard Categories	Nonsacramental uses counted in other categories
Religion	$ 12.49	$ 10.26
Health	3.68	3.98
Education	3.57	4.41
Social Welfare	1.61	2.07
Arts, Humanities, Civic and Public	1.54	1.67
Other	2.69	3.19

†*Giving in America,* p. 58.

But most of the giving to religion is in relatively small amounts. The contributors are often not as concerned about external incentives for giving—such as tax deductibility—as they are about supporting their church. And lower-income people give a much higher proportion of their philanthropy to religion than do upper-income people: in 1972, 70% for those with incomes under $10,000 and 66% for incomes between $10,000 and $20,000, compared with 7% for those with incomes over $200,000. This amounted (in 1970) to $63 for the year from the person making less than $5,000; $138 for the person between $5,000 and $10,000; $191 for the next bracket, and so on.[4]

The philanthropic support of other charitable undertakings tends to be dominated to a much greater degree by "big givers" for whom philanthropy is a more self-conscious process: they often seek out the recipient from whom they will derive: (a) the maximum tax deductibility, (b) the most visibly "humanitarian" results, (c) the greatest

4. *Giving in America,* p. 59.

respect, renown, or notoriety, (d) the longest and broadest perpetuation of influence, name, and reputation, or (e) a combination of the above. As a result, they tend to concentrate on universities, hospitals, libraries, museums, opera houses, and symphony orchestras, which can more readily become monuments to their memory in the community at large (though there are "memorial" churches as well, to be sure), and much of their giving is in "single-shot" benefactions or endowments which make a heavy impact at one time but are not the humble week-by-week, year-after-year support such as churches attract. (This is true even though big givers can spread the single large gift over several years for tax purposes.) Bequests, foundation grants, and corporate giving also tend to go to nonreligious purposes. (In a recent period, only 4% of foundation grants went to religion and only one-third of one percent of corporate giving.[5])

The point of the foregoing survey is to suggest that the pattern of giving upon which churches depend is significantly different from the pattern of giving in the rest of the charitable sector. It consists predominantly of many small gifts in a steady flow rather than being dominated by a few large nonrecurring ones, and those continuing small contributions come primarily from adherents. Mandatory disclosure in connection with charitable solicitations is designed to protect the giving public from fraud and exploitation, but this protection is both less necessary and more intrusive in the case of religion than in other areas of philanthropy. That is, in the great bulk of giving to religion, the recipient organization is a church, and it is already quite well known to most of its contributors. They do not need the help of a disclosure law to "protect" them from their own church. Their knowledge is more intimate and their remedy more direct than law can provide. If they are not satisfied with the conduct of the church's affairs, they can work within it for reform or betake themselves and their contributions to some more satisfactory church. Also, with respect to churches, disclosure is not as necessary to protect "big givers" not personally familiar with the recipients of their largesse, since churches do not normally expect large gifts from nonadherents (and not many from adherents).

5. *Ibid.* p. 60.

The possibilities of fraud in the fund-raising efforts of churches, then, are considerably less than in other areas of philanthropy. And if it does occur, government is not necessarily in a position to recognize or rectify it, since one person's "fraud" may be another's "faith." Government does have an obligation to detect and punish crimes such as extortion, larceny, embezzlement, or misrepresentation of securities, but these are not the misconduct designed to be prevented by mandatory disclosure in charitable solicitations. The typical target of disclosure is the shyster or confidence man who raises charitable contributions under false pretenses—using little or none of the proceeds for the charitable purpose announced. The counterpart in the religious realm would presumably be the charlatan who sets up a sham religion and raises money for it from gullible contributors. The classical case of this type is the "I Am" movement which gave rise to *U.S.* v. *Ballard.*

Guy W. Ballard, Edna W. Ballard, and Donald Ballard were indicted and convicted for using the mails to defraud. They claimed to have access to "Saint Germain" and various "ascended masters" who imparted to them supernatural knowledge, including the ability to heal (and cause) diseases. The Ballards apparently attracted followers on the strength of these claims and appealed for contributions to the public by mail, which brought about their indictment. The government charged that the Ballards "well knew" that their claims were false, and promulgated them only to deceive and defraud. Although the trial judge instructed the jury that they could not assess the truth or falsity of the Ballards' teachings or beliefs, but only their sincerity, the jury convicted them. The U.S. Supreme Court agreed that the jury had no business testing the truth of religious doctrines. Mr. Justice Douglas, writing for the Court, summed up the situation:

> Freedom of thought, which includes freedom of religious belief, is basic in a society of free men. It embraces the right to maintain theories of life and of death and of the hereafter which are rank heresy to followers of the orthodox faiths. Heresy trials are foreign to our Constitution. Men may believe what they cannot prove. They may not be put to the proof of their religious doctrines or beliefs. Religious experiences which are as real as life to some may be incomprehensible to others. Yet the fact that they may be

beyond the ken of mortals does not mean that they can be made suspect before the law.

The Fathers of the Constitution were not unaware of the varied and extreme views of religious sects, of the violence of disagreement among them, and of the lack of any one religious creed on which all men would agree. They fashioned a charter of government which envisaged the widest possible toleration of conflicting views. Man's relation to his God was made no concern of the state. He was granted the right to worship as he pleased and to answer to no man for the verity of his religious views.[6]

The Court remanded the case for the disposition of other issues raised by defendants but not decided by the lower court. One Justice, Robert H. Jackson, felt that the jury should not even have been asked to assess the sincerity of the Ballards; calling their teaching "humbug," he offered the following forthright dissenting views:

William James, who wrote on these matters as a scientist, reminds us that it is not theology and ceremonies which keep religion going. Its vitality is in the religious experiences of many people. "If you ask what these experiences are, they are conversations with the unseen, voices and visions, responses to prayer, changes of heart, deliverances from fear, inflowings of help, assurances of support, whenever certain persons set their own internal attitude in certain appropriate ways." If religious liberty includes, as it must, the right to communicate such experiences to others, it seems to me an impossible task for juries to separate fancied ones from real ones. . . .

There appear to be persons—let us hope not many—who find refreshment and courage in the teachings of the "I Am" cult. If the members of the sect get comfort from the celestial guidance of their "Saint Germain", however doubtful it seems to me, it is hard to say that they do not get what they pay for. . . . The chief wrong which false prophets do to their followers is not financial. The collections aggregate a tempting total, but individual payments are not ruinous. I doubt if the vigilance of the law is equal to making money stick by over-credulous people. But the real harm is on the mental and spiritual plane. There are those who hunger and thirst after

6. *United States* v. *Ballard,* 322 U.S. 78 (1944).

higher values which they feel wanting in their humdrum lives. . . . When they are deluded and then disillusioned, cynicism and confusion follow. The wrong of these things, as I see it, is not in the money the victims part with half so much as in the mental and spiritual poison they get. But that is precisely the thing the Constitution put beyond the reach of the prosecutor, for the price of freedom of religion or of speech or of the press is that we must put up with, and even pay for, a good deal of rubbish.

Prosecutions of this character easily could degenerate into religious persecution. I do not doubt that religious leaders may be convicted of fraud for making false representations on matters other than faith or experience, as for example if one represents that funds are being used to construct a church when in fact they are being used for personal purposes. But that is not this case. . . . I would dismiss the indictment and have done with this business of judicially examining other people's faiths.[7]

What the "Constitution put beyond the reach of the prosecutor," it has also put beyond the reach of the examiner. It is not the duty or responsibility of government to intervene between churches and their adherents in order to scrutinize and standardize and certify their fund appeals. (That is a different thing from responding to complaints of misrepresentation, misuse of funds, violation of fiduciary trust, etc., against whomever charged, including religious leaders.)[8]

The principle of governmental noninterference is expressed in the Internal Revenue Code at Section 7605(c), "Restriction on Examination of Churches." When the Tax Reform Act of 1969 was being debated in the U.S. Senate, Senator Wallace Bennett (R-Utah) expressed the concern that, in providing for the taxing of church income from unrelated trade or business, the Act might encourage the Internal Revenue Service to intrude into the internal affairs of churches.

MR. BENNETT: Mr. President, the other amendment refers to what I think is a desirable clarification of the language in the bill which, for the first

7. *Ibid.*
8. Where the fund appeal or charitable solicitation is carried on for the church by a professional or commercial fund-raiser, however, he or she should be subject to registering, licensing, reporting, and/or disclosure requirements of "Truth-in-Giving" laws.

time, allows the Internal Revenue Service to audit churches. This has not been possible under the previous law. . . .⁹

The "Bennett Amendment"—now part of the Code—reads as follows:

> No examination of the religious activities of such an organization [a church or convention or association of churches] shall be made except to the extent necessary to determine whether such organization is a church or a convention or association of churches, and no examination of the books of account of such an organization shall be made other than to the extent necessary to determine the amount of tax imposed by this title [on unrelated business income].¹⁰

This section of the Code applies to taxable years beginning after January 1, 1970. The earlier portion of Section 7605(c) provides that an audit to determine whether a church owes tax on its unrelated business income may be initiated only with the approval of "a principal internal revenue officer for an internal revenue region" with advance written notice by him to the church.

The plain, though convoluted, language of the Bennett Amendment, when combined with Senator Bennett's explanation of his intention at the time, seems clear. Governmental tax examiners are not to go rummaging through the internal affairs of churches, and certainly not through their religious activities. Counsel for the National Council of Churches has taken the view that the Bennett Amendment simply expressed the law already existing, though the Internal Revenue Service has in the past occasionally audited churches and church organizations. This matter was brought to a head when the Internal Revenue Service undertook to audit the National Council of Churches in 1970. When asked the scope and purpose of such audit, IRS replied:

> Unlike the examination of business corporations, in which the focus is primarily upon examination of receipts and expenditures and the determination of taxable income, the examination of exempt organizations, because compliance with the conditions of their exemption must be

9. Congressional Record, S 15951, December 6, 1969.
10. Section 7605(c).

verified, requires an audit of virtually all the organization's activities, including its records and evidence of programs, publications, and personnel functions.[11]

At no time during several years of discussion between IRS and NCC did the former indicate any awareness that the courts had implied that churches, conventions, and associations of churches were to be treated with more care than business corporations. Instead, IRS was claiming a vastly more sweeping responsibility to scrutinize churches and other exempt entities than it claimed with taxpayers! During the course of this altercation—which ended with the NCC consenting to an examination for years prior to 1970 and the IRS at last returning a clean bill of health—the Treasury promulgated regulations for the implementation of Section 7605(c) which reduced its effect to virtually nothing. Despite protests from NCC and other religious groups, the regulations are now in effect, and Senator Bennett's amendment is, in effect, nullified.

Nevertheless, it is in the law, and churches, conventions, and associations of churches might do worse than to assume that the law means what it says, despite the regulations. They should consider resisting any attempt by IRS to audit them except for unrelated business income, and only to the extent of that income.

Although churches themselves should not be required by law to disclose their internal financial affairs, they should have no reluctance to do so voluntarily. Even more important, they should be impeccably scrupulous in the use they make of money contributed for religious and charitable purposes. Such contributions represent a trust which is in some instances legally enforceable and in all cases morally binding upon the recipient church to use the money, insofar as possible in accordance with the contributors' wishes.

This brings us to a very subtle but important problem: not all contributors' wishes are consonant with the church's purposes or the character of a genuine charitable contribution, and churches must be equally scrupulous in observing those considerations. Contributors sometimes give money to churches with "strings attached"

11. Letter, District Director to R.H. Edwin Espy, General Secretary, NCC, May 4, 1971.

that would distort or dilute the church's purposes. Suppose an elderly woman gave her church $100,000 to set up a trust fund, the income of which was to be used to provide a home and continuing care for her favorite cats and all homeless cats within ten miles of the church, up to the capacity of the fund. It is doubtful that the church would want to be drawn by this gift into devoting significant time and effort to the administering of a veterinary institution, however benignly intended. The contribution would be "charitable" enough—if made to the ASPCA—and the church's purposes are broad enough or vague enough that almost anything could be covered by them, but does the church *want* to spread its wings so broadly? One would like to think that most churches would ask themselves, "How does that activity advance the cause of Christ?" —or some such question—and have the integrity sometimes to say, "No, thanks." If churches do not protect their own integrity, who will do it for them? The government?

It is regrettable that sometimes the scrutiny of government seems more effective in recalling a religious body to its appropriate purposes than do the scruples of its members (as in the cases noted at the beginning of the chapter). In this respect, as in other church-state relations, if churches were more vigorously aware of their own unique character and function, there would be less need for legal strictures. (This is not meant to justify subjecting churches to mandatory disclosure laws or routine governmental audits or inspections; only where there is probative indication of deliberate fraud should government attempt to intervene.)

The Internal Revenue Code defines a "charitable contribution" (for purposes of deductibility from taxable income, Section 170(c)) primarily by the *organization* to which it is given and only secondarily by the *use* to be made of it. The main category of *organizations* to which deductible contributions can be made are the organizations described in Section 501(c)(3), and the *purposes* for which charitable contributions may be made are the same as the purposes of organizations in that category: "religious, charitable, scientific, literary, educational, or for the prevention of cruelty to children or animals" (Section 501(c)(3) includes one other purpose, "testing for public safety"). In addition, "charitable contributions" by corporations to a trust, chest, fund or foundation are deductible only if used within the United States or any of its possessions.

Thus it is the church or other charitable organization which—in the first instance, at least—confers deductibility upon contributions. (If it is subsequently shown that they were not actually used by the organization for charitable purposes, then presumably deductibility would be revoked, and the taxpayer who had claimed it would have to pay the requisite tax on the amount of contribution incorrectly deducted.) This does not happen very often, particularly with churches, whose contributors are less likely to make large gifts or to be as heavily motivated by deductibility. But church leaders, in determining whether to accept larger contributions and how to use them, should be doubly vigilant, not only to protect the purposes of the church, but to avoid being inadvertently "used" to confer deductibility upon contributions that are not really "charitable."

The situation which should trigger such vigilance is an approach by a contributor who wishes to make a substantial gift to the church for a specific, "designated" purpose. Suppose Mr. Flush wants to give the church $10,000 to assist a struggling public-interest law firm in the neighborhood that is working hard to help poor tenants to get adequate heating and repairs from slum landlords. He is not related to the two young lawyers who comprise the firm, and he will not derive any personal profit or income from his gift—other than the satisfaction of helping a cause he believes in. The public-interest law firm is not itself tax-exempt, though it has applied for an exemption and is probably entitled to it, but the Internal Revenue Service scrutinizes such applications very carefully, in some cases until the applicant has succumbed.[12]

If Mr. Flush is in the 50% tax bracket, his gift will cost him only $5,000—*if* he can deduct it from his taxable income—because he would have to pay the other $5,000 in taxes anyway. If it is deductible, the second $5,000 goes to the benefit of the young lawyers rather than to Uncle Sam. And even though it "costs" Mr. Flush only $5,000, it will buy a full $10,000 worth of supplies for them. (That is what is

12. Under the Tax Reform Act of 1976, however, for the first time organizations which have lost exemption or have not obtained a ruling from IRS can get a declaratory judgment from the courts (Section 7428).

meant by "soft" money, but it buys just as much as "hard" money.)

Should the church accept the proffered gift with the designation attached to it? If Mr. Flush is a former or potential contributor to the church, the urge to oblige him will be strong. The church has long had a humane concern with the plight of the poor in its vicinity, and has several ongoing programs designed to help them, including a day-care center, a tutoring service for high school dropouts, and a tenants' complaint-referral exchange (which advises callers what department of the city administration or what private agency is most likely to be able to help them). It would look with favor on the kind of work being done by the public-interest law firm in question, but had never heard of it until Mr. Flush brought it to the church's attention.

The church's policy-making board investigates the situation and concludes that neither Mr. Flush nor the young lawyers seem to have ulterior motives. The board likes what it learns about the law firm's work, and feels that its purposes are entirely consonant with what the church is already trying to do for slum tenants and other poor people in the vicinity. If the church had an extra $10,000, it might well use it to aid the new law firm, and so it assures Mr. Flush that it will do so. He gives the money. The church makes a grant of $10,000 to the law firm. And Mr. Flush claims a $10,000 charitable deduction on his income tax. What will the Internal Revenue Service do?

Normally, most such deductions are not challenged if they are not obtrusively large for the donor's income—or the recipient's. If this transaction were to be scrutinized, however, it might well be disallowed on the grounds that the church did not really choose how to use the money. Mr. Flush specified how it was to be used, and the church merely acquiesced. Therefore, the two young lawyers were actually the recipients rather than the church, and contributions to them are not deductible. From the moment it assured Mr. Flush that it would accede to his wishes, the church was acting merely as a "conduit" and could convey no genuine charitable deduction.

This interpretation of the situation is based on the few court decisions in this rather undefined area of tax law. In one case, a taxpayer contributed for several years to a tax-exempt orphanage to maintain a particular child, of whom he had been a foster parent for several years. His contributions were ruled by the Tax Court to be in effect a gift to the child and not really "to or for the use of" the orphanage and therefore not deductible.

> They were earmarked from the beginning not for a group or class of individuals, not to be used in any manner seen fit by the society, but for the use of a single individual in whom petitioner felt a keen fatherly and personal interest.[13]

A Revenue Ruling by the Internal Revenue Service refers to a taxpayer who contributed to the missionary fund of his church while his son was a missionary receiving money from that fund. The ruling held the contributions to be deductible because the church rather than the donor decided how the money would be spent:

> If contributions to the fund are earmarked by donor for a particular individual, they are treated, in effect, as being gifts to the designated individual and are not deductible. . . . The test in each case is whether the organization has full control of the donated funds, and discretion as to their use, so as to insure that they will be used to carry out its functions and purposes.[14]

In another case, a taxpayer had been contributing to the Sudan Interior Missionaries for twenty years, writing on each check the names of the same four missionaries. The Mission, however, had announced that all funds it received would be pooled each month and divided equally among all its missionaries. The Tax Court held that the Mission exercised sufficient discretion in the distribution of the funds to prevent the donations from being personal gifts to the named missionaries.[15]

Of course, that is what happens in any large charitable organization when gifts are received designated for particular programs or purposes within its existing budget. Unless they exceed the amount already allotted to a given item, no change in the budget is necessary; undesignated funds are simply deployed to cover other items not favored by donors with earmarked contributions. This may seem unfair to donors whose "pet" projects get no extra funds despite

13. *S. E. Thomason,* 2 T.C. 441 (1943).
14. Rev. Rul. 62–113, 1962, 2 Cum. Bull. 6.
15. *George E. Peace,* 43 T.C. 1 (1964).

their designated gifts, but it is the way the organization preserves its discretion to manage its own internal affairs in such a way as to fulfill its purposes, without which contributions to it are not properly deductible anyway. If one project is getting a disproportionate amount of designated gifts to the detriment of the rest of the organization, the organization would have to consider declining the designated contributions in order to preserve its own internal symmetry and integrity. Or it should accept all designations with the proviso that the organization will use its discretion in applying them to its purposes.

Another quality which must be present for contributions to be considered genuinely charitable and thus deductible is illustrated by a recent decision regarding a fund set up to benefit the survivors and families of victims of the sinking of a particular ship on one of the Great Lakes. The court held that the beneficiaries formed too small a class to endow the fund with the "requisite indefiniteness" essential to true charity.[16] Perhaps a fund for "Shipwrecked Seamen on the Great Lakes" might have been broad enough to qualify.

This case only underlines the point that contributions for individually identifiable beneficiaries are not "charitable" and therefore not deductible. Yet it is individually identifiable persons whose plight makes the most moving appeal for contributions. This paradox is seen in *The New York Times*'s annual campaign for "New York's Neediest Cases," which raises large sums of money every year by publishing the sad tales (with pictures) of a number of individual cases. Yet the money received does not actually go directly or solely to the relief of the cases described but to the social-welfare agencies from whose files the cases were drawn. Some of the contributions do undoubtedly benefit the publicized cases— along with many others.

If donors deduct their contributions to such causes from their taxable incomes, it would be on the supposition that any designations they may have made were "precatory" rather than "mandatory" upon the recipient agency—advice or suggestion rather than command. Any check sent in with a letter saying the donor would like it to be

16. *Schoellkopf* v. *U.S.*, 124 F.2d 982 (2d Circuit, 1942).

used "to help the sweet little girl whose picture appeared in yesterday's *Times*" cannot be deducted if the donor expects the designation to be taken literally. Of course, it isn't. One could say that the benefit of that check did indeed go to the little girl in question, but an equivalent amount of undesignated funds that would have gone to her was redirected to other cases that would have gotten a share of the check if it had not been designated.

Most large-scale fund appeals of this type, which bring in many small contributions from donors for whom deductibility is not a major consideration, state, imply, or assume that any designations are "precatory" and not binding on the organization so long as it uses the funds for its general charitable purposes. One attorney advises all clients seeking incorporation of charitable organizations to include in their charters an article stipulating that all contributions received —whatever their designation—will be used at the discretion of the organization to carry out its charitable purposes.[17]

Such a stipulation may cover the legal problem, but it does not necessarily solve the moral and public-relations problems. Suppose a church were to launch a special fund drive to provide a Christmas party for every inmate in a nearby mental institution, and the cause was so appealing and the drive so successful that the amount needed was vastly oversubscribed. What should the church do with the excess? In this blessed but unlikely eventuality, it would seem that the church would want to follow the same trust principle *(cy pres)* that applies when a testator's purposes cannot be carried out: the bequest must be used for the next nearest *(cy pres =* "so near") or most similar purpose available. The balance—after the party has been paid for very generously— should not just be "remaindered" into the church's treasury, however meritorious the church's general purposes are thought by its members to be, since nonmember contributors may be left with the impression that money given for a specific (external) cause was used to build up the church itself (internal)—which may not have been at all what they intended. A more suitable disposition in this instance would be to provide some additional service or benefit to

17. William J. Lehrfeld, in oral comments at a Consultation of Churches and Tax Law, George Williams College, Williams Bay, Wisconsin, October 21, 1975.

the inmates who were the intended beneficiaries of the fund drive.

In any event, it should be clear that the purposes of the church are defined, determined, and implemented by the decisions of its policy-making body and not by contributors or the tax code. Whether it be the vestry, the session, the clergy, or the whole congregation or membership, the policy-determining body of the church should be very jealous of its task and very conscientious in performing it. They should want to take full and sole responsibility for defining the church's purposes, embodying them in various activities and programs, and finding the resources to finance them. To do so, they can solicit, receive, and expend contributions for all or parts of the church's work, and those contributions will be presumed to be deductible because they are for the furtherance of the church's purposes—by definition.

The church can also "farm out" various elements of its work to other agencies, persons, or entities equipped to do it, whether they are members or full-time employees of the church or not, whether they are tax-exempt or not—so long as the church retains "discretion" as to how its funds are used and control over their usage.

A church might set itself these limits in soliciting and receiving deductible contributions for designated purposes:

1. Contributions will not be received that are designated for non-exempt third parties;
2. Contributions will be received designated for particular purposes, programs, or projects of the church itself, which have been duly authorized in advance as part of its religious activity by the appropriate internal body;
3. Expenditure of such contributions for the purpose designated will be entirely within the discretion of the church or its appropriate internal body;
4. If the church cannot find a way to utilize such contributions within its own purposes and the donor's designation, it will return the donation to the donor with an explanation of the problem;
5. The church will determine the best means of carrying out its purposes with such contributions, and if an outside agency is utilized will

continue to exercise expenditure accountability to make sure that its funds are applied to its purposes by any contractor, agent, or grantee.[18]

A church that knows what it is doing and why will be less susceptible to intimidation by government or exploitation by outsiders with ulterior motives. It will also be a more effective religious body.

18. Dean M. Kelley, "Churches and the Internal Revenue Code" (mimeographed paper for distribution to church leaders, New York: National Council of Churches, August 31, 1971), pp. 26–27.

9

Ministers Pay Taxes

Some people seem to be under the impression that members of the clergy do not pay taxes as other citizens do. That impression is erroneous, and it is worth digressing for a few pages to correct it. Yet there are some differences in their tax liability and that of other citizens that deserve attention. The basic point to be made is that, with a few minor exceptions, the ordained clergy of the churches do not personally benefit from the exemption of churches from taxation, but pay taxes like anyone else. If they own property, they pay property taxes on it in most jurisdictions (minus an allowance of $1,500 on the assessed valuation of such property in New York State—providing the clergy person is engaged full time in church work). If they have income, they pay income taxes on it. (Members of religious orders who have taken a vow of poverty do not have personal income from services they perform on behalf of their orders and so do not pay taxes on compensation they receive for such services.)

For some curious reason, members of the clergy are categorized for income tax purposes as "self-employed" and are not subject to withholding of income tax because their income is defined as not constituting "wages,"[1] even though it may be paid by a church that in other respects looks much like an "employer." As a consequence, the member of the clergy must pay the entire Social Security tax rather than

1. Section 3401(a)(9) of the Internal Revenue Code.

having the employer pay part of it—a difference of 2.05% in the amount of tax paid on maximum income taxable for Social Security.

In addition, "ministers, members of religious orders, and Christian Science practitioners" may exempt themselves from payment of the tax on "self-employment income"—and from any consequent benefits under the Social Security Act—if they are "conscientiously opposed to . . . the acceptance of . . ." such benefits.[2] Both laity and clergy may be exempted from such tax if they are members of "a recognized religious sect" which eschews social insurance and looks after its own members' needs in old age and disability.[3] (This is an exemption designed to benefit the Old Order Amish, whose horses and other property were seized by the Internal Revenue Service to pay their Social Security tax, which they neither needed nor used, as they are conscientiously opposed to relying on government for the care which they believe the religious community should provide.)

The one significant advantage which the clergy enjoys in respect to income taxation is the mandatory exemption of "the rental allowance paid to him as part of his compensation, to the extent used by him to rent or provide a home."[4] This provision is an extension of the principle that the *rental value* of a residence furnished by the church is not to be calculated as part of the clergy's income. Since some churches do not provide a parsonage or rectory but simply pay a cash housing allowance to enable the clergyperson to rent or buy a residence, it might seem reasonable to count that allowance also as not being taxable income. The basic principle is not much different from the treatment afforded any employee whose employer furnishes lodgings as a condition of employment.[5] The president of a university who lives in an official residence on campus or the superintendent of a hospital who lives in a staff house on the grounds enjoys this consideration, as does the factory watchman whose compensation includes a small room where he lives on the premises or the maid or butler who resides in the "servants' quarters." A preacher who dwells in a parsonage adjacent to the church is in no very different situation. Even

2. Section 1402(e).
3. Section 1402(h).
4. Section 107(2).
5. Section 119.

a parsonage not contiguous to the church is comparable, since church committees and classes may meet there.

But the housing allowance paid in cash is an extension of the principle significantly beyond what is available to lay persons, particularly if the clergyperson is not serving a local congregation but is employed as a denominational executive or a seminary professor in a position that could be held by a layperson. In a large denominational headquarters, some bizarre anomalies are created when ordained persons receive an amount designated in advance each year by the employer as "housing allowance," which need not even be declared as income, while non-ordained persons performing the same or comparable tasks at equivalent salaries must pay income tax on the full amount. (It was precisely this type of contrast which was called to the attention of the courts by Dr. W. Astor Kirk, a political scientist employed by the then Board of Christian Social Concerns of the Methodist Church. He contended that it was unjust and unconstitutional that he be taxed more than an ordained person doing the same kind of work in the same office at the same level of compensation, but the court simply stated that he did not qualify for the cash housing allowance exemption afforded by Congress.[6] Of course, Kirk did not want to qualify for it; he wanted it struck down as unconstitutional.)

As a matter of fact, it is not easy to qualify for that exclusion. The regulations governing Section 107 are very explicit. The cash housing allowance exclusion is available only if:

1. It is authorized in advance of the tax year by official action of the employer, stipulating a certain amount (not a percentage of salary), which can be amended later if the actual amount expended was more or less than that stipulated (though there are probably not many instances in which the amount is amended downward).

2. The recipient employee is duly ordained, licensed, or certified by the church or synagogue (in this usage, a rabbi qualifies as a "minister of the gospel"!; a "minister of music" or "minister of religious education" does not qualify).

3. The ordained person is employed full-time "in the exercise of his ministry"—a qualification that has led to some very interesting

6. *Kirk* v. *Commissioner,* 51 T.C. No. 8 (1969), 425 F.2d 492 (D.C. Cir.), *Cert.* denied, 400 U.S. 853 (1970).

encounters with the Internal Revenue Service.

The Service has disallowed the claims of some ordained persons to exclusion of cash housing allowance from taxable income on the ground that they were working in positions which the Service did not consider to be "in the exercise" of their "ministry." A Methodist minister working as a chaplain of an industrial mission under an appointment by his bishop had his housing allowance taxed. So did a Baptist minister working for a Christian Action Council in a southern state—the equivalent of a state council of churches—until he confronted IRS with a favorable ruling it had given another clergyman employed by the State Human Rights Commission—a governmental agency.

Normally, IRS tends to accept the definition of religious "ministry" represented by the appointment or designation of a bishop, but denominations not having bishops are at a disadvantage in authenticating their more unconventional ministries. One Baptist clergyman who was actually commissioned by his denomination as a missionary to serve as director of a church-supported agency to encourage and fund self-empowerment and community organization among minorities had his housing allowance taxed, and his denomination prepared to go to court to win recognition of the validity of its definition of ministry, but the Internal Revenue Service backed down.[7]

Surely the government should not be in the position of trying to determine what is "in the exercise" of a clergyperson's religious "ministry," and what is not, but that anomaly is the result of an improper classification in the law, which benefits only ordained persons. It is an example of special privilege that is difficult to justify, and the National Council of Churches has urged its elimination—thus far without success:

> Employees or other functionaries of religious organizations—lay or clergy
> —should not enjoy any special privilege in regard to any type of taxation.
> A clergyman properly pays his income tax as other citizens do. If he
> receives a cash allowance for housing, that amount should be taxed as part

7. See an excellent paper on this subject, "In the Exercise of His Ministry," by Earl Trent, House Counsel, Division of National Ministries, American Baptist Churches, Valley Forge, Pa., n.d.

of his income, as it is for laymen. . . . Whether the value of housing provided a clergyman by his church should be taxed is a question that should be resolved as part of the broader category of all employees who occupy residences furnished for their employer's convenience.[8]

Some commentators in the law journals consider the exclusion of cash housing allowance for ordained clergy patently unconstitutional.[9] As long as it exists in the law, however, it should not be arbitrarily granted to some clergy and denied to others on the basis of whether IRS believes their "ministry" to be religious. If Section 107 were to be repealed or struck down by the courts as unconstitutional, IRS would be spared the sticky and inappropriate responsibility of trying to define religious "ministry" in non-hierarchical bodies.

8. Policy statement TAX EXEMPTION OF CHURCHES, May 2, 1969.
9. Roger H. Taft, "Tax Benefits for the Clergy: The Unconstitutionality of Section 107," 62 *Georgetown Law Journal* 1261 (1974).

10

Can Churches Lose Exemption?

The threat of loss of tax exemption or deductibility or both has been used increasingly by government of late as a means of inducing certain kinds of behavior or inhibiting others on the part of exempt organizations. Private schools set up to avoid racial integration were found by a three-judge court to be operating contrary to "federal public policy" and therefore not entitled to a "charitable" exemption,[1] and the Internal Revenue Service has since required all private schools to affirm and publicize a racially nondiscriminatory policy in order to gain or keep tax exemption.[2]

The court did not explicitly apply its rule to *religious* private schools, but it did glance in their direction:

> The special constitutional provisions ensuring freedom of religion also ensure freedom of religious schools, with policies restricted in furtherance of religious purpose. . . . We are not now called upon to consider the hypothetical inquiry whether tax-exemption or tax-deduction status may be available to a religious school that practices acts of racial restriction because of the requirements of religion. Such a problem may never arise; and if it ever does arise, it will have to be considered in the light of the particular facts and issue presented, and in the light of the established rule,

1. *Green* v. *Connally,* 330 F. Supp. 1150 (D.D.C., 1971), affirmed sub nom. *Coit* v. *Green,* 404 U.S. 997, (1972).
2. Rev. Rul. 71–447, C.B. 1971–2, 230, Rev. Proc. 72–54, C.B. 1972–2, 834. Cf. Form 1023.

see Mormon Church v. U.S. . . . that the law may prohibit an individual from taking certain actions even though his religion commands or prescribes them.[3]

Just as the claim of religious freedom did not enable the Mormons to continue to practice polygamy, so it would not justify racial discrimination in private schools operated by religious groups, the court seems to conclude.

A few years later, the Internal Revenue Service informed Bob Jones University that it would have to drop its ban on admission of blacks or lose its tax exemption. But Bob Jones University sought an injunction to prevent such action by the government, maintaining that *exclusion of black students was required by the religious doctrines governing the school*—the hypothetical situation the *Green* court had envisioned. The suit was decided, not on the merits, but on the procedural point that an injunction could not be obtained to forestall a tax ruling. Bob Jones University would have to pay the tax and sue for a refund in order to get into court—which could take years and thousands of dollars—even if it won in the end.[4] Rather than undergo that struggle—or apprehensive that it might not prevail on the merits in the end—Bob Jones University capitulated and decided it could admit black students after all, just as the Mormon Church, after years of litigation, decided it could forego or suspend the religious requirement or doctrine of "plural marriage."

Some people may feel a sense of satisfaction that these religious groups were persuaded to abandon their "antisocial" practices, but one may wonder whether it is not a rather limited concept of religious freedom which allows the government to intervene in the faith-inspired practices of a religious group—however benighted—for reasons less compelling than imminent actual threats to public health or safety. Whose religious obedience will the government deem "antisocial" tomorrow?

Thus far the threat of loss of tax exemption has not been applied to churches which discriminate on the basis of race in admission to

3. 330 F.Supp. at 1169.
4. *Bob Jones University* v. *Connally,* 416 U.S. 725 (1974) affirming 472 F.2d 903 (4th Cir. 1973). But note that a declaratory judgment can now be obtained in loss-of-exemption cases under Section 7428, Internal Revenue Code.

membership in the church itself. The Mormon Church, for instance, does not admit blacks to the "higher priesthood"—a "lay" office to which most male members of the church aspire—though it does not exclude them from membership. The President, Chief Seer, and Revelator of the Church insists that this is a matter of divine command and cannot be abridged by human will until the Lord issues a new command—as He thoughtfully did, via President, Chief Seer, and Revelator Wilford Woodruff, back in 1890, permitting the Saints to relax the practice of plural marriage which was causing them so much trouble at that time.

The Black Muslims have recently rescinded their ban on white members, but would they have lost their tax exemption if they didn't? Is a religious group entitled to draw its membership solely from one race, or to exclude a particular race—or several—from membership? If not, why not? In a free society, the ultimate power, if not the only power, which churches possess to protect their purpose, their doctrine, their integrity, is the "power of the gate"—the ability to determine who can get in and stay in. The church is essentially an exclusive community, which must be able to admit those who adhere to its tenets and obey its requirements and to exclude those who do not. That is the first and most fundamental prescription of religious liberty.

Granted, some may say, but what has that to do with *race?* A church could insist on the most rigid standards of faith and behavioral conformity without arbitrarily shutting out some potential members because of their race. But that is not the point here. Are "outsiders" to tell a church how to select its members? Is the government to set standards for how churches operate? Are the Black Muslims not entitled to limit their membership to black people if they wish? (The exclusion of the "white devils" may have been one factor contributing to their intense morale and drive; their willingness now to admit whites seems like a "loss of nerve" comparable to the Mormons' willingness to abandon "plural marriage" or the Oneida Community's relinquishment of "complex marriage"—a lowering of the "cost" of adherence which maintains a religion's convincingness.)

Could a religion from the Far East not limit its membership to Asians, or a cult of American Indians to Native Americans? (None of them does, but is it impermissible?) Every religion must be able to separate the "sheep" from the "goats" and to define "goats" and "sheep" as it sees fit. Anything less than that strikes at the roots of religious liberty. If that sweeping but essential insistence be granted, we may take some reassurance from the fact that Christianity and most other world religions do *not* exclude any category of converts on the basis of "involuntary" traits—those a person did not choose and cannot change: race, sex, age, place of birth. Actually, churches *do* discriminate against some persons on the basis of such traits: as by refusing to admit into full membership anyone under the age of fourteen, for instance. And some exclude women from certain leadership positions—a topic treated below. Various ethnic churches tend to limit their membership—in practice, at least—to persons of the same national origin, but this may be done, not so much by banning non-Serbians from the Serbian Orthodox Church, for example, as by holding services in that Serbo-Croat language, which only members of that ethnic group can understand. (Actually, their services are in Old Church Slavonic, which no one can understand!)

Probably the loss of tax exemption will not be applied as a sanction against churches which deny *membership* to various (seemingly arbitrary) categories of people—though it *has* been applied to fraternal lodges which excluded certain races from membership. But fraternal lodges do not have the claim to religious liberty that churches have. Some may insist that "religious liberty" should never be used to justify actions that are bad, but who is to define "bad"? Certainly "religious liberty" would not justify murder or robbery or other acts that threaten public health or safety, but considerations of public order or public policy are at a lower level of urgency, and religious liberty should take precedence over them, and in a number of more recent Supreme Court decisions, it has.[5] This is said, not to condone or encourage discrimination, but to emphasize the importance of religious liberty.

But the sanction of loss of tax exemption may be invoked in certain instances against churches or church agencies which discriminate in *employment* (rather than membership), so let us turn to that more

5. *Sherbert* v. *Verner,* 374 U.S. 398 (1963), *Wisconsin* v. *Yoder,* 406 U.S. 205 (1972).

limited area. Title VII of the Civil Rights Act of 1964 prohibits discrimination in employment by private employers, but provided (in its original form) an exemption for religious groups:

> Section 702. This subchapter shall not apply to . . . a religious corporation, association, or society.

But Senator Hubert Humphrey added an amendment which limited the exemption as follows:

> Section 702. This subchapter shall not apply to . . . a religious corporation, association, or society with respect to the employment of individuals of a particular religion to perform work connected with the carrying on by such corporation, association, or society of its religious activities. . . .

Thus religious groups were permitted to discriminate solely for the purpose of hiring their own members and solely for carrying out their *religious* activities.

In 1972, when the Act was amended, Senator Sam Ervin tried to restore it to its original form, so that "the Equal Employment Opportunity Commission would have no jurisdiction at all over religious institutions," but his effort failed by a vote of 25 to 55. He did succeed, however, in getting the word "religious" deleted as a modifier of "activities," so that the section as amended now reads:

> Section 702. This title shall not apply . . . to a religious corporation, association, educational institution, or society with respect to the employment of individuals of a particular religion to perform work connected with the carrying on by such corporation, association, educational institution, or society of its [   ] activities.

(Note the addition of "educational institution" and the assumption that the "particular religion" to be hired will be the organization's own religion—probably a safe assumption—but the actual wording of the law would not exclude a Baptist Church from employing only Sikhs because of their abstemiousness!)

However, a three-judge panel of the U.S. Court of Appeals for the District of Columbia Circuit unanimously characterized the Ervin deletion of the word "religious" in Section 702 as an unconstitutional violation of the Establishment Clause of the First Amendment and of the Due Process Clause of the Fifth, since it carves out a special exception from the Civil Rights Act of 1964 solely for religious organizations, permitting them to discriminate in employment, not only with respect to their religious activities—which the court considered constitutional—but with respect to *all* activities, including commercial ones.[6] Fortunately or unfortunately, depending upon one's point of view, the Civil Rights Act itself was not before the court at the time, so Section 702 as last quoted above remains for the time being the law of the land.

The options logically available to religious groups with respect to possible discrimination in employment would seem to be as follows:

1. They can discriminate *on any basis* (not only religion but sex, age, race, national origin, class, intelligence, marital status, right-handedness, etc.) in employment *in any capacity* (preacher, secretary, janitor, etc., regardless of how remote from "religious activity). This was the preference of Senator Ervin, but he lost.

2. They can discriminate only *on the basis of religion* (and then only in favor of "a particular faith"—presumably their own) in respect to employment *in any capacity.* This is the gist of the present Civil Rights Act of 1964 as amended by the Equal Employment Opportunities Act of 1972, containing the one-word deletion on which Senator Ervin won.

3. They can dicriminate *on any basis,* but only in employment closely involved *in carrying out distinctively "religious activities."* This was the view of the *King's Garden* court, above, and the *McClure* court, below.

4. They may discriminate only *on the basis of religion* and then only for *carrying out religious activities.* This was the import of the Humphrey amendment to the Civil Rights Act of 1964 prior to the Ervin deletion in 1972.

5. They may not discriminate *on any basis* in respect to *any position of employment.* There appears to be no significant proponent of this view.

These options can be arranged on a two-dimensional chart, with one dimension representing the *basis* of discrimination (any basis,

6. *The King's Garden* v. *FCC,* 498 F.2d 51 (5th Circ, 1974).

religion only, or none) and the other representing the *activities or positions* in which such discrimination can be exercised (in respect to *all* activities or only in respect to *religious* activities).

MAY DISCRIMI-NATE:	ON *ANY* BASIS	ON BASIS OF *RELIGION* ONLY	ON NONE
IN RESPECT TO *ALL* ACTIVITIES	1. Ervin	2. Present Act	5. (Null)
IN RESPECT TO *RELIGIOUS* ACTIVITIES ONLY	3. *King's Garden* and *McClure*	4. Previous Act	

The only case dealing directly with these questions in depth (at the present writing) is *McClure* v. *Salvation Army*. Mrs. Billie McClure was an officer (commissioned clergyperson) of the Salvation Army (a church). She had received several years of specialized training for this work and had been employed as the spiritual leader of local "corps" or congregations of the Salvation Army in Little Rock, Arkansas, and Pascagoula, Mississippi. Later she was employed by the Army in "staff" positions as a case-work supervisor and as a secretary in public relations at the Georgia (regional) headquarters of the Salvation Army—in all of which positions, she testified, she considered herself to be performing religions duties.

Gradually she became disenchanted with the Army's differential treatment of woman officers as compared with men officers, particularly the lower pay and dependency allotments for women. When she complained about these inequalities, she was scheduled for a hearing to review her fitness to be an officer in the Army. Thereupon she went to the Equal Employment Opportunity Commission (Senator Ervin's *bête noire*) in Atlanta and filed a formal complaint against the Salvation Army, which promptly suspended her and then terminated her employment altogether. Mrs. McClure then went to court.

The U.S. District Court for the Northern District of Georgia held that Mrs. McClure had been performing "religious activities" (even though some were similar to secular activities) for a religious body, and that persons in such roles were not covered by the Civil Rights Act. The U.S. Court of Appeals for the Fifth Circuit did not agree, contending that the Act forbade religious groups to discriminate in employment on the basis of sex, race, or national origin—thus seeming about to vindicate Mrs. McClure. But then the court went on to say that in so legislating, Congress was interfering in the internal relationships between a church and its clergy, which it has no power to do. In order to avoid declaring the law unconstitutional, however, the court construed it to mean that "Congress did not intend . . . to regulate the employment relationship between church and minister,"[7] thus deciding *against* Mrs. McClure. (The U.S. Supreme Court declined to hear the case.)

In this decision, the determinant of permissible discrimination by religious bodies is not *per se* the religious nature of the activities in which the employee is to engage but the *ordained status* (or equivalent) of the employee—perhaps on the assumption that the clergy are by definition engaged in "religious activities." Mrs. McClure's loss is a gain for the free exercise of religion: the right of churches to define their own character and choose their own leadership without governmental interference.

That right may soon be put to the test again in respect to the refusal of some churches to ordain women to the priesthood. William Stringfellow, attorney for one of the "irregularly" ordained women priests of the Episcopal Church, has threatened to take that church to court for sex discrimination in employment, but it is hard to see how he would avoid the wall that blocked Mrs. McClure: the reluctance of courts—and imputedly of Congress—to interfere in the relationship between a church and its clergy. (The more recent action by the General Convention of the Episcopal Church permitting women to be regularly ordained as priests may have rendered this particular controversy moot, but other churches may face similar challenges in the near or distant future.)

There may be those who will say, "Any church may exclude any

7. *McClure* v. *Salvation Army,* 460 F.2d 553 (5th Cir., 1972), *cert.* denied, 409 U.S. 896 (1972).

group it wants to; it just can't do it with the help of a tax exemption!" That is precisely the kind of statement that was made by the Tenth Circuit Court of Appeals in regard to Billy James Hargis: he is perfectly free to influence legislation as much as he wants, but not with a tax exemption.[8] The same rationale could be applied to any activity on the part of churches that is displeasing to the government or the majority of the population. It can be used as an ever-present club to keep the churches in line—*if* it is something the courts or legislators or administrators can give or take away at will. (The legislature of California once tried to require churches to take a loyalty oath every year to qualify for tax exemption—until the U.S. Supreme Court struck down the statute, not because the legislature couldn't take away the tax exemption—alas!—but because the state had the burden of proving *dis*loyalty rather than citizens or churches having the burden of swearing loyalty.[9]

As stated earlier, even if tax exemption is no more than a privilege granted by the legislature (which is not conceded), it cannot be "given" to churches on the condition of abandoning rights guaranteed by the Constitution—whether that be the right to assemble freely and petition the government for redress of grievances, or the right to admit members and select leaders on whatever basis seems divinely required. If the threat of loss of tax exemption can be used as a club to keep churches "in line," it will work in the same direction as establishment (discussed in Chapter 4), benefitting the churches which are "constructive," "responsible," "respectable," or "loyal," while penalizing those that are "antisocial," "fanatical," "irresponsible," or "uncooperative"—that is, precisely the churches which have greatest attractiveness to, and greatest effectiveness with, the oppressed, the alienated, the anomic, the outcasts of society—who most need religious help if the health of society as a whole is not to be endangered.

It is the thesis of this book that tax exemption is not something churches (or any nonprofit voluntary organizations, for that matter) win by "good" behavior or lose by "bad" behavior, as "good" or "bad" may be defined at will by incumbent officials from day to day.

8. *Christian Echoes National Ministry* v. *U.S.,* quoted in Chapter 6.
9. *First Unitarian Church* v. *Los Angeles County* 357 U.S. 545 (1958), *Speiser* v. *Randall,* 357 U.S. 513 (1958). See Appendix A.

Churches have their essential function to perform, which they do—and have done for decades and centuries—as best they can, and which outsiders, particularly government officials, cannot judge, and—even if they could—do not have the wisdom, means, or right to try to improve the churches' performance. Loss of tax exemption will not make poorly functioning churches function better, and the threat of it will only have a "chilling effect" on those that are not doing too well as it is, so that they will tend to falter and "lose their nerve" and do even less well.

Tax exemption is not something to be turned on and off like a spigot, but an optimum, constant condition for allowing the religious function to be performed in a "free market" situation, where would-be practitioners are allowed to "sink or swim" on the basis of how well they meet the religious needs of adherents—without governmental interference, either to hinder or to "help" (which is still to hinder). One does not have to be a partisan of one religion or of any to appreciate and wish to maintain this commendable "hands off" neutrality of government toward religion, which the First Amendment commands, and which tax exemption so excellently epitomizes.

Appendix A

Digest of Important Court Decisions on Tax Exemption

This appendix lists and describes, in chronological order, some of the key court cases that have become landmarks in the field of tax exemption. The citations refer to the annual reports of various courts. "U.S." refers to the series of *United States Reports* containing the decisions of the U.S. Supreme Court. "F.2d" refers to the *Federal Reporter, Second Series,* containing the decisions of the Circuit Courts of Appeals. The number preceding the title is the volume number; the number following is the page number.

Slee v. *Commissioner of Internal Revenue,* 42 F.2d 184 (2d Circuit, 1930). Noah Slee claimed a deduction from his federal income tax for contributions made to the American Birth Control League. Because that organization included among its activities the attempt to ease the legal barriers to the dissemination of birth-control information, Judge Learned Hand held that it was not exclusively charitable, and therefore the contribution to it was not deductible. See page 22.

Girard Trust Co. v. *Commissioner of Internal Revenue,* 122 F.2d 108 (3d Circuit, 1941). The issue in this case was whether a bequest to the Board of Temperance, Prohibition and Public Morals of the Methodist Episcopal Church was charitable, inasmuch as that agency urged legislation prohibiting sale of alcoholic beverages. The court held that these activities of the Board "fell within the type which have been regarded as religious by the Methodist Church for a century and a half," and seeking to have its views enacted into law did not render them other than religious, therefore "charitable," and deductible.

Seasongood v. *Commissioner of Internal Revenue,* 227 F.2d 907 (6th Circuit, 1955). A former mayor of Cincinnati sought to deduct contributions made to the Hamilton County Good Government League, which he had served as president for twelve years. The League devoted "less than one-twentieth" of its efforts to attempting to influence legislation, and the court held that this was not a "substantial" amount, thus allowing the deduction. (It is from this decision that the supposed figure of 5% as the IRS measure of "substantiality" derives, but a larger figure might also have passed the court's scrutiny.)

Speiser v. *Randall,* 357 U.S. 513, and *First Unitarian Church* v. *County of Los Angeles,* 357 U.S. 545 (1958). These are companion cases arising under a 1954 California law requiring all applicants for tax exemption to subscribe to a loyalty oath. Speiser, a World War II veteran, and the First Unitarian Church (among others) refused to sign the oath and were denied the exemption. The U.S. Supreme Court struck down the statute as a violation of due process of law because it placed the burden of proof (of loyalty) upon the applicants rather than upon the state (to prove disloyalty). (The Court did not reach the Church's claim of violation of religious liberty but decided its case on the same due-process grounds as the veteran's.)

Cammarano v. *U.S.,* 358 U.S. 498 (1959). Two liquor dealers, one in Washington and one in Arkansas, contributed to efforts of their industry to defeat statewide initiatives that would have eliminated their businesses and then claimed the contributions as deductible business expense. The deduction was disallowed on the ground that Treasury regulations clearly excluded expenditures for supporting or opposing legislation from deductible costs of doing business. (The significance of this Supreme Court ruling is that Congress amended Section 162 of the Internal Revenue Code a few years later to make such expenditures, in certain circumstances, deductible for businesses.)

Walz v. *Tax Commission,* 397 U.S. 664 (1970). A taxpayer sued the tax collector for refund of that portion of his property taxes that he would not have had to pay if churches were taxed, since exempting them from property taxation, he contended, is an "establishment of religion" prohibited by the First Amendment. The Supreme Court held that the New York State Constitution, in exempting religious, as well as educational and charitable, property from taxation, had not violated the no-establishment clause. See page 20.

Green v. *Connally,* 330 F.Supp. 1150 (D.D.C., 1971), affirmed *sub nom. Coit* v. *Green,* 404 U.S. 997 (1972). In this case, testing whether private schools admitting white students only are eligible for tax exemption, a three-judge court found that "charitable" does not cover racial discrimination because it is contrary to "federal public policy," and therefore IRS should obtain proof of racial non-discrimination before granting exemption. (The court explicitly refrained from deciding the question of *religious* private schools claiming to practice racial exclusion as a religious requirement, which was not before it.)

Christian Echoes National Ministry v. *U.S.*, 470 F.2d 849 (10th Circuit, 1972), *cert.* denied, 414 U.S. 864 (1973). Billy James Hargis, an ultra-conservative radio preacher, lost his tax exemption for engaging to a substantial degree in attempting to influence legislation. The Tenth Circuit rejected his claim that his religious liberty had been impaired, holding that he was still free to preach on legislative issues, but without a tax exemption (!). See page 79.

Appendix B

Church Views on Tax Exemption

"The United Methodist Church and Church-Government Relations in the U.S.A."

Adopted by the General Conference
of the United Methodist Church, May, 1968

V. *A Statement Concerning Church-Government Relations and Tax Exemption*

1. "We believe that governments recognize the unique category of religious institutions. This unique category is not a privilege held by these institutions for their own benefit or self-glorification but is an acknowledgement of their special identity designed to protect their independence and to enable them to serve mankind in a way not expected of other types of institutions.

2. "It is our conviction that the special treatment accorded to churches and conventions or associations of churches with respect to exclusion of their unrelated business income from income taxation ought to be discontinued.[1] We believe there is no justification for relieving churches of the obligation of reporting their earnings in the same manner that is required of charitable organizations.

"We urge churches to consider at least the following factors in determining their response to the granting of immunity from property taxes:

"1.   Responsibility to make appropriate contribution, in lieu of taxes, for essential services provided by government;

[1. It was discontinued in the Tax Reform Act of 1969.]

"2. The danger that churches become so dependent upon government that they compromise their integrity or fail to exert their critical influence upon public policy.

3. "We support the abolition of all special privileges accorded to members of the clergy in American tax laws and regulations, and call upon the churches to deal with the consequent financial implications for their ministers. Conversely, we believe that all forms of discrimination against members of the clergy in American tax legislation and administrative regulations should be discontinued. We believe that the status of an individual under ecclesiastical law or practice ought not to be the basis of governmental action either granting or withholding a special tax benefit."

"Relations Between Church and State"

Adopted by the 175th General Assembly of the
United Presbyterian Church in the U.S.A., 1963

9.   *Tax Exemption for Religious Agencies*

The church has no theological ground for laying any claim upon the state for special favors. The church must regard special status or favored position as a hindrance to the fulfilling of its mission. As a matter of contemporary fact, various levels of government give the church and many of its agencies a wide variety of tax exemptions. The church would find it difficult to obtain the abrogation of these laws and administrative practices. In the face of this situation, two points need to be made abundantly clear by the church, the first directed to itself and its membership and the second to the state and its representatives.

First, to itself as the agent of the ministry of Jesus Christ to the world, the church should know that it renders its witness ambiguous by its continued acceptance of special privileges from the state in the form of tax exemptions. Second, the state should know that it may not expect from the church in return for favors extended of its own free will, any *quid pro quo* in the form of a muting of the church's prophetic voice, nor should the state expect the church to accept the role of an uncritical instrument of support for the state's programs, or of any other conscious dilution of its supreme loyalty to Jesus Christ.

In view of these considerations, the Special Committee on Church and State *recommends* that:

a.   United Presbyterians study the nature of our Church's involvement in economic activity and seek ways by which it can begin the process of extricating itself from the position of being obligated, or seeming to be obligated, to the state by virtue of special tax privileges extended to it.

b.   The United Presbyterian Church carefully examine its national and local related business enterprises to assure itself that under present tax laws these enterprises are not unfairly competitive with secular businesses operating in the same fields. To this end the Committee suggests that the General Assembly direct the Stated Clerk to canvass the boards, agencies, institutions, and judicatories to determine the extent of their economic involvement subject to tax exemption and to report to the General Council of the United Presbyterian Church, which is to report to a future General Assembly.

c.   The United Presbyterian Church continue efforts to obtain repeal of the section of the Internal Revenue Code that allows "churches and church organizations" exemption from the corporate income tax on profits from businesses unrelated to the purpose or activity of the church or church organization.

d.   Congregations be encouraged to take the initiative in making contributions to local communities, in lieu of taxes, in recognition of police, fire, and other services provided by local government. This consideration commends itself especially to well-established and financially stable churches and particularly in those communities where tax problems are developing due, in part, to the increase in exempted properties for all purposes—educational, governmental, charitable, and religious. Those congregations which thus make voluntary contributions in lieu of taxes should not expect consideration or special favor in return.

10.   *Special Privileges for the Clergy*

It must be recognized that many special privileges are given to the clergy, but most of these fall within the realm of the traditional attitudes of the public concerning the clergy and do not directly concern the relationship between the church and state and thus are outside the mandate. The principal example of a special privilege granted by the state to the clergy consists of certain favorable tax treatment. Special tax exemptions for ministers are not different in principle from special tax exemptions for religious institutions.

The Special Committee on Church and State, therefore, *recommends* that this question be considered in the light of the previous recommendation (Section 9).

"Religion and Public Policy"
> Adopted by the Baptist Joint Committee on Public Affairs
> (encompassing nine Baptist conventions), October 7, 1975

WHEREAS, Section 501(c)(3) of the federal Internal Revenue Code establishes a category of religious and nonreligious public charities which are exempt from federal income taxation, and

WHEREAS, that Section of the Code provides that no ". . . substantial part of the activities [of a public charity may consist of] attempting . . . to influence legislation," and

WHEREAS, donors to those public charities whose legislative activities are held to be substantial will not receive a tax deduction for their contributions, and,

WHEREAS, the Internal Revenue Service has applied an uneven measure of "substantiality" in dealing with Section 501(c)(3) charities and appears to us to have used the test for political reasons, and

WHEREAS, many religious organizations hold that a part of their religious mission is to give witness to their religious beliefs as they affect or are affected by public policy, and

WHEREAS, the state has never had constitutional power to determine, direct, or limit religious programming for churches, associations of churches, or conventions of churches but currently is authorized to do so indirectly through the substantiality test of 501(c)(3), and

WHEREAS, the First Amendment puts religion in a unique and specially protected category, and

WHEREAS, it is an accepted legal doctrine that the state may not require an individual or an organization to forego a constitutional right to qualify for the statutory benefit, and

WHEREAS, churches have not accepted and cannot accept the substantiality test without violating deep religious beliefs,

BE IT THEREFORE RESOLVED, That the Baptist Joint Committee on Public Affairs in its meeting on October 7, 1975 respectfully requests that the Congress of the United States specifically exempt churches, associations of churches, or conventions of churches from the substantiality test of 501(c)(3) or any modification of that Section;

BE IT FURTHER RESOLVED, That the Committee directs its staff to use all appropriate means to oppose any modification of 501(c)(3) which does not exempt any organization protected under the religion clauses of the First Amendment from the substantiality provisions of that Section.

TAX EXEMPTION OF CHURCHES

A policy statement of the National Council
of the Churches of Christ in the United States of America;
adopted by the General Board, May 2, 1969

The following policy statement is an attempt to deal in non-technical terms with a limited area of tax policy which has a limited effect upon the well-being of society. It is not an attempt to assess the wider and more important ranges of general tax policy, where glaring inequities and gaping loopholes call for moral scrutiny by the churches at the earliest opportunity.

No brief outline of general principles can do justice to the many unique situations in which the churches seek to minister to minority groups or special populations. If the principles set forth below should have an adverse effect upon any small, struggling churches in the inner city, the rural parish or the Indian reservation, or if the changing nature of the mission of the church should necessitate changes in the traditional concepts of tax-exemption, these policies, like the tax-codes themselves, are subject to revision by subsequent actions.

Christians are advised in Gospel and Epistle to pay their proper taxes to the governing authorities (Matthew 17:24, 22:19, Romans 13:6). Their obedience to God normally includes the obligation to pay their just share of the cost of public order, justice and service which God has appointed the authority of government to provide. Since this advice applied to an imperial Roman regime, how much more apt it is in respect to a government in which the citizens have a voice in the imposition and disposition of their taxes. Although individual Christians for reasons of conscience sometimes refuse to pay a particular tax, in general we recognize and uphold the power of taxation as the necessary mechanism by which the resources of society are directed to the ordering of its life and the solution of its problems.

The New Testament does not deal directly with taxation of Christians in their corporate activities, but its recognition of government's rights to tax has implications for the church as a corporate structure in the modern world.

1.   *Churches should ask of government (for themselves) no more than freedom and equality.* For all members of society, Christians expect government to establish and maintain justice, order, defense, welfare and liberty, recognizing that in a democracy they and all others share in the responsibility which government discharges. They can also ask that the tax laws be administered and enforced fairly, equitably and expeditiously for all. For themselves and their churches, however, Christians ask no more from government than freedom to proclaim and bear witness to the Gospel: to preach, to teach, to publish, to worship and to serve in obedience to the will of God as it is made known to them. They ask of government protection of this freedom rather than direct support of their activities. Churches can ask exemption from taxation only if it is essential to protect their freedom or to afford equal treatment among them.

2.   *Tax exemption can be a safeguard of the free exercise of religion.* In the United States, it has been a basic public policy since the founding of the nation to accord to freedom of religion, speech, press and assembly a "preferred position" at the head of the Bill of Rights. Christians support and affirm this healthful arrangement of the civil order, not solely or primarily for themselves and their churches, but for everyone. Citizens, whatever their beliefs, should likewise appreciate the policy of our society that the free exercise of religion cannot be licensed or taxed by government. Property or income of religious bodies that is genuinely necessary (rather than merely advantageous) to the free exercise of religion should likewise not be taxed. Except for cases where exemption is required to afford equality with other eleemosynary institutions, such exemption should be confined to the essential facilities of the church and to the voluntary contributions of the faithful for the operation of the religious organization.

Such exemption has usually been regarded as a benefit but not a subsidy (in the sense of a cash outlay). There is no doubt that an organization is financially stronger with a tax exemption than without it, but the exemption does not convey to the organization funds it has not already attracted from voluntary contributors on its own merits. That is, a church cannot be built with a tax exemption alone. It is built by the donations of its adherents because they believe in its purposes. Exemption from taxation merely permits full use of their gifts for these purposes without drawing off a portion for the purposes of the whole society, which the members already support directly through the taxes they pay as individual citizens.

3. *Government may encourage voluntary organizations through tax exemption.* Society is stronger and richer for the voluntary associations in which citizens voluntarily band together for constructive purposes independent of government support and therefore of government control. Exemption from taxation is one way in which government can and does foster such voluntary groups.

Christians may agree with other citizens in the civic judgment that it is good public policy not to tax non-profit voluntary organizations. Though they may view religious organizations (especially their own) as something more than "nonprofit voluntary organizations," they may concede that it is an appropriate category in which government may classify them. If religious organizations are so classified and so exempted, they do not thereby enjoy any "special privilege" that is not shared with a broad range of generally meritorious secular groups.

4. *Tax exemption may entail conditions which Christians cannot accept.* Society may extend exemption from taxation to religious organizations on the condition that they meet certain tests, such as subscribing to loyalty oaths or refraining from political activity. Whatever may be the civil merits of this policy, Christians must determine independently whether the acceptance of such conditions will hinder their obedience to the will of God, and, if so, dispute the conditions. If tax exemption will tend to curtail or inhibit their efforts to affect public policy, churches may want to set up non-exempt agencies for political activity, using contributions that are not deductible.

5. *Taxation on real property of religious organizations.* Depending upon the exigencies of the total tax base, states and municipalities may be more or less generous in exempting the property of religious and other non-profit voluntary organizations from taxation. Parsonages and parking-lots are taxed in some localities but not in others, at the discretion of the legislature. Religious organizations have accommodated themselves to a wide range of such provisions over the centuries, and will continue to do so. They should not begrudge paying taxes on auxiliary properties to help defray the costs of civil government. Certainly no exemption from property taxes should be sought for property owned by religious organizations which is not used primarily for religious (or other properly exempt) purposes.[2]

2. Property obtained for expansion or relocation of churches (and the income derived therefrom, if any) may be exempted for a reasonable period of time until the church can expand or relocate on it.

Churches should be willing to pay their just share of the cost of municipal services which they receive, such as fire, police, and sanitation services. Some do this through voluntary payments "in lieu of taxes"; others might offer to pay service charges for the particular services they use.

6. *Deductibility of contributions to religious organizations.* At present, citizens may deduct from their taxable income certain gifts and contributions to a wide variety of "charitable" organizations—religious, scientific, literary, humane, educational, etc. Where it is public policy to encourage contributions to voluntary nonprofit organizations in this way, religious organizations need not be arbitrarily excluded from that classification, nor given preferential treatment. If it becomes public policy not to allow deductibility for contributions, religious organizations should not claim a special privilege of deductibility.[3]

7. *Taxation of employees of religious organizations.* Employees or other functionaries of religious organizations—lay or clergy—should not enjoy any special privilege in regard to any type of taxation. A clergyman properly pays his income tax as other citizens do. If he receives a cash allowance for housing, that amount should be taxed as part of his income, as it is for laymen. Likewise, if he owns his own home, he should not enjoy any reduction of property taxes which is not equally available to his unordained neighbor. In case of a cash allowance, only the non-recoverable costs, which do not include payments on principal, should be included; if property taxes and interest are included in the allowance, they should not also be claimed as deductions.

Whether the value of housing provided a clergyman by his church should be taxed is a question that should be resolved as part of the broader category of all employees who occupy residences furnished for their employer's convenience. Equity might be better served if the dollar equivalent of all such housing was taxed as income. In localities where parsonages are exempt from school taxes, provision should be made by local churches for payment of tuition or the equivalent. Whatever the solution, churches should compensate their employees for any losses incurred through the elimination of special privileges from the tax laws. We favor legislation requiring payment by churches and church agencies of the employer's contribution to social security tax for both lay and clerical personnel (except those bound by a vow of poverty).

8. *Unrelated business income.* Churches constitute one of the few categories of otherwise tax-exempt organizations which do not pay taxes on the income

3. An existing statement by the General Board of February 27, 1963, supports the deductibility of charitable contributions and opposes a "threshold" on such deductions.

from business enterprises they own which are unrelated to their exempt purpose. Churches should not be in a position where they are tempted to "sell" their exemptions to businesses seeking a tax advantage over taxpaying competitors. Therefore we urge that federal tax law be revised so that any "church or convention or association of churches" which regularly conducts a trade or business that is not substantially related to its exempt function shall pay tax on the income from such unrelated trade or business.[4]

9. *Disclosures.* If they engage in unrelated business enterprises, churches should be required to file full financial reports with respect thereto. Even if not so engaged or required, it is good policy for churches voluntarily to make available to the public a complete, audited annual report of income and expenditures, assets and liabilities, so that there is no mystery about the nature and extent of their operations.

4. This revision could best be made by deleting from Section 511 of the 1954 Internal Revenue Code the parenthetical expression: "(other than a church, a convention or association of churches)," and making suitable provision as to "business lease" rental income which is debt-financed.

Those changes would not affect dividends, interest, annuities, royalties, capital gains, or rents from real property (except as already indicated).

We would not object to a delay of up to five years in applying such taxes to businesses now held by churches, nor to a "floor" deduction large enough to permit trivial or transitory activities by churches which do not rise to the level of serious competition with taxpaying trade or business.

The definitions and descriptions of "trade or business" "regularly," "conducts," and "substantially related" in Treasury Regulations, Paragraph 3256, seem generally reasonable and equitable, and do not appear to threaten the legitimate exercise of religious freedom if applied to churches.

Index